D1035598

MAKE EVERY WORD COUNT

Cincinnati, Ohio

MAKE EVERY WORD COUNT

A guide to
writing that works – for
fiction and nonfiction

Gary Provost

Excerpt from "Las Vegas (What?)" from *The Kandy-Kolored Tangerine-Flake Streamline Baby* by Tom Wolfe. Copyright © 1964 by Tom Wolfe. Reprinted by permission of Farrar, Straus and Giroux, Inc.

Excerpt from *Wild Times.* Copyright © 1978 by Brian Garfield. Reprinted by permission of Simon & Schuster, a division of Gulf & Western Corporation.

Make Every Word Count. Copyright 1980 by Gary Provost. Printed and bound in the United States of America. All rights reserved. No part of this book may be reproduced in any form or by any electronic or mechanical means, including information storage and retrieval systems, without permission in writing from the publisher, except by a reviewer who may quote brief passages in a review. Published by Writer's Digest Books, 9933 Alliance Road, Cincinnati, Ohio 45242. First edition.

Library of Congress Cataloging in Publication Data
Provost, Gary, 1944-
    Make every word count.
    Includes index.
    1. Authorship. I. Title.
PN145.P7   808'.02   80-23699
ISBN 0-89879-020-4
ISBN 0-89879-040-9 (pbk.)

Book design by Barron Krody

Because she walked with me every step of the way to all those empty mailboxes, this book is dedicated to my wife Nora (aka Pumpkin), whom I love more.

ACKNOWLEDGMENTS

Though a writer might hate to admit it, writing a publishable book is not something he does all by himself. He might write an almost publishable book, but by the time he is done his brain has become temporarily useless. Then he needs people to point out that his logic is sometimes circular, his metaphors are often mixed, his modifiers now and then dangle, and what he has written clearly and concisely he has written clearly and concisely six times.

Those people are called editors, and I have four of them to thank along the way. At Writer's Digest Books they are Carol Cartaino, who knew exactly what I was talking about and encouraged me to write it down, and Howard I. Wells III and Anne Montague, who edited the final manuscript. But before they ever saw it, I had to write it, and that can be a lonely business. Fortunately, I had another editor, Donna Scalcione-Conti, who is a freelance writer and my most valued friend. Donna read the book as it came along, six or seven pages at a time, and she told me that it was good but still, this sentence could be improved and that paragraph could be cut. And best of all, she wrote "good" here and there in the margins, which, of course, is why I kept writing more pages.

To all of them, my thanks.

CONTENTS

Part 6: Description That Works

Part 7: Points of View

INTRODUCTION

We are writers, you and I.

We are writers because we write.

I have written over six hundred articles and stories that were published. I have written two books that were published.

But I have also written six books that were not published. And I have written hundreds of story beginnings, incomplete poems, bits of dialogue, and assorted great ideas that were never published.

It is what I have written that makes me a writer, not what I have published. If you write, you are a writer, whether you have published millions of words, a very few words, or no words at all.

I never had a word of mine published until I was twenty-nine, but I was a writer long before that. Writing has always been part of my life. Through practice and observation I've come to learn what writing works and what doesn't, and I'd like to share that with you.

When I was eight years old I put out a daily newspaper which I printed on yellow composition paper in the shed of our Boston home. The neighbors used to pay me a nickel a copy, so I guess the writing worked.

When I was fourteen I wrote long threatening letters to the credit manager of the Columbia Record Club. He was always sending me notices, suggesting I pay for the albums I had ordered. I was quite broke, so I always wrote back telling him not to walk through any dark alleys on the way home.

"You'll hear the heavy, ominous footsteps of a madman," I once wrote, "the chilling, insane laughter, the blood-curdling shriek, and the sickening thud of the mighty sledgehammer coming down on your head."

As you can see, I exercised considerable writer's license in these letters, for it seems safe to say that should one be brained by a deranged teenager wielding a sledgehammer, one would not hear the thud. Anyhow, his letters stopped coming. The writing worked.

I kept a writer's journal on and off during my teenage years, and even after I got out of high school and hit the road for a year of hitchhiking around the USA, I used to scrawl out story ideas on paper bags between rides.

After two years of rambling I stopped in New York City. I got an exciting job as a delivery boy for a watch importer, rented a microscopic apartment on the west side of Manhattan, and dished out fifty bucks for a secondhand typewriter. I was ready to become a writer.

Like most writers, I delved first into my own experience. I began a novel called *The Rabbit Knows*, which was about my hitchhiking experiences. I was like a lot of beginning writers. I thought the way to write a book was to load it up with a lot of words I had never seen in any other book.

One paragraph of *The Rabbit Knows* begins "So he stood torpidly on the pebbled border of the lifeless highway, with his arm outstretched across the corroded asphalt, and his thumb sought some sort of concession to his distress, and once again he found himself making nugatory conjectures.''

It whipped right along like that for fifty pages or so before I wore out my dictionary and canceled the whole project. The writing didn't work.

Fortunately for me, in New York I was lonely, scared, shy, friendless, and incapable of dialing a female's phone number. I also didn't have a television set. So, of course I had to do some writing. I also read books about writing. I took a few creative writing courses, and I picked up the latest issues of the writer's magazines during lonely walks up Broadway. I started dozens of stories and novels, finished a few. Slowly my writing improved. It could hardly have gotten worse. Eight years later I made my first sale. I'm thirty-five now, and for the past six years I've made all of my living from writing, editing, or teaching about writing. Millions of people read the words I write. Editors send me checks. The writing works.

I'm telling you something about myself so that you will feel you know me. It's important that the reader know and like the author, and you should always strive to make yourself likable in your writing. If you like me you will be more inclined to read what I write, just as you would listen to a friend's tales of prizes won and dreams gone sour sooner than you would listen to a stranger's. While you will rarely present yourself in your work as I have here, you will always be there as the author. Later I will be talking about agreements made between authors and readers, but for now you should know there is always a covenant between the writer and reader, a covenant based on trust and affection, and if there is one thing you should ''feel'' about me through this book, it is this: I am on your side.

Also, by sharing some of my experience with you I have made myself a specific person. If I had jumped right in with some writing rules I would come across like the insensitive boss who shows up at the office barking orders without stopping to say good morning. I would be a disembodied voice, easy for you to ignore. But I am an individual now, someone you can see, someone you can hear, someone who is almost in the room with you telling you these things. When we discuss characterization later in the book, you'll see how important it is to make your people, whether they are real or fictitious, individuals.

I've also told you some of my writing background so that you would see that getting published is something that happens to unpublished writers. That fact might seem as obvious as leaves on a tree, but for a good many unpublished writers there is a mysterious gap between the unpublished and the published. They don't think it, but they *feel* that these are two unrelated groups, not recognizing the former as the pool from which the latter is drawn.

I was like that. Before I started selling my writing, the whole thing was a mystery to me. What exactly do checks from publishers look like, I wondered. Would I understand a book contract? It's easy for me to laugh at myself now, but at the time these questions were painfully real.

There is a difference between published and unpublished writers, but it is one of degree, not an absolute. Publication is not some magical turning point after which you suddenly know all there is to know about writing. It is more a measure of your progress toward an imaginary point of writing perfection (which, of course, can never be reached).

My goal in this book is to bring you a lot closer to that point. The difference between you and me, if you are a beginner, is not that I have learned some secret code word and been welcomed into an exotic world of professional writers. The difference is simply that I have put in more time at it, written more words, and in doing so have learned to make my words count. This is not a book about being a writer. It is a book about writing that works.

Part

ONE

Some Questions Answered

Can Writing Be Taught?

No. Throw this book away.

Yes, yes, of course writing can be taught.

I'm not sure why this question keeps coming up, but it does. People ask it of me and all writers, at parties and bus stops, and I feel like replying, "Geez, I dunno. I didn't use to know how to write good but now I do, so yeah, I s'pose it can be taught."

My wife Nora plays the guitar, and nobody has ever asked her if guitar playing can be taught.

Anyhow, yes, writing can be taught. This assumes a certain basic understanding of language, just as the teaching of accounting assumes an ability to add and subtract. It's true that some people will never get the hang of writing well, just as some people never get the hang of riding a bicycle. There are always exceptions. But good writing, writing that works, does contain observable, repeatable phenomena, and the person who has noted them can "impart knowledge or skill; give instruction; provide knowledge of; cause to learn by example or experience." Those are my dictionary's definitions of *teach*.

However, to teach writing one must first make some arbitrary distinctions. A piece of writing is not like a car, for example, where something is either a carburetor or a spark plug, no matter how you hold it or where you view it from. You can't unscrew and yank out one part of writing and drop it in a bag without dragging along chunks of all the other parts, but for the purposes of teaching writing we pretend that you can do just that.

If I wanted to teach you how to make a car, it would not be enough just to march you down to your local Ford dealer and have you stare through the showroom window at a new red Mustang. I'd have to throw open the hood, rip off the doors, thresh out every screw and wire in that car, and lay the parts across the floor. Then I would have to piece them all back together again so that you could see how the car was made. In fact, I would have to do this several times for you to understand.

So to teach you to write, I'll pretend that it's like a car as I break writing down into parts called *description*, or *dialogue*, or *style*. But because writing is not really like a car, the part that I call *style*, for example, won't look exactly like the part that another author or teacher calls *style*.

Just as the word *piece* is a verb in one sentence in this section, and a noun in another, any collection of words can be many different parts of writing, depending on how you look at it.

Consider this sentence:

"Beneath the lefthand pocket of his corduroy jacket, bulging like a tumor, was the pearl-handled revolver Leo always carried out of fear that Chinese bandits were going to kidnap him."

Think about that pearl-handled revolver for a minute. What element of writing is it? Is it description? Is it style? Is it characterization?

It's all of them, depending, as I say, on how you look at it.

It is description, because the pearl handle gives you a color and a texture to see, and the shape of the revolver creates a memorable bump that will summon to mind the larger picture of Leo. It is style, because I said *revolver* when I could have said *gun*, or *pistol*, or *piece*, all of which would have given you a slightly different sense of the weapon. The pearl-handled revolver is also characterization, since it embodies the raging paranoia that is one of Leo's character traits.

So when you make the right choices, every word will count, and if you've just learned that, then you know for sure that writing can be taught.

What Do You Mean by "Writing That Works"?

By writing that works, I mean writing that does the job it's supposed to do, whether that job is to inform, entertain, sadden, anger, or instruct. Writing does not work if it only entertains when it is supposed to instruct. It does not work if it only angers when it is supposed to educate. Whether a piece of writing has been put together to convey factual information or to create images in a story, it should be judged not on good grammar or adherence to the rules of composition (both of which are tools, not goals), but on how well it does its job. Does it work? Does this word reveal my character's feeling? Does this sentence convey the popularity of stock car racing? Does this paragraph communicate the feeling of despair these refugees have?

For any given idea there exists a variety of technically and grammatically correct word combinations that can be used to communicate it. But each word combination alters the idea. It is the form the writer chooses, the words he picks out, that determine the content of his work, what he really says, and whether or not the writing works. For example, here are two grammatically correct sentences about the same fact:

1. The twenty-seven-year-old father of three little boys died last Friday afternoon in an accident at work.

2. Twenty-seven-year-old Hubie Humwicker drowned Friday afternoon when he tumbled into a 300-gallon vat of chocolate syrup.

Both sentences are accurate and readable, but I controlled your reaction to the information by the facts and words I chose to use, and the writing in either sentence is good only if it is consistent with the effect I wanted. With the first sentence I wanted you to feel sad for three kids. In the second sentence I wanted you to smile. If I had wanted you to feel sad and yet still told you about the vat of chocolate syrup, the writing would not have worked.

Writing that works is also writing that assigns a job to every word in a sentence. Every word, every sentence, every paragraph must be doing some work or it should be fired. You don't need a pink slip. You need a blue pencil or a large wastebasket.

The writing that has worked in the past is an enormous body of evidence we can sift through for clues to good writing. The successful writers of today, the ones who are getting published and cashing checks, are those who recognize what made someone else's writing work. Writing that works is writing that works every day for the average professional writer. With that in mind, my examples will not be extracted exclusively from the works of Nobel Prize winners and dead Russian novelists.

What, No Hemingway?

If you go into the library and thumb through books about writing (the 808 section in a Dewey decimal system library; the P section if it's on the Library of Congress system), you'll find that most authors proffer a bit of advice and then wheel out the excerpts from Fyodor Dostoevski and Ernest Hemingway to prove the advice is sound. While it's nice to know some great writers have honored some good rules of writing, it's more important to realize that these rules have worked for published writers in general. So, with all due respect to Ernest Hemingway, his work will not be appearing in this book.

Downstairs I have a large bookcase containing around three hundred books—paperbacks, mostly. They range from six-dollar college editions to coverless pulps that went four for a buck at the 7 Eleven. Among them are bestsellers such as Irving Wallace's *The Plot*, and James Michener's *Centennial*; books that were made into movies, such as *Dog Day Afternoon* by Patrick Mann; and books that can't be filmed, such as *Getting Things Done* by Edwin C. Bliss. This motley collection includes fiction, like James Kirkwood's *Some Kind of Hero*, and nonfiction, like Alan Moorehead's *The White Nile*. There are books like *Marilyn* by the famous Norman Mailer and books like *Son of*

The Great American Novel by the not so famous James Fritzhand. No logic, no pattern shapes this collection. It represents nobody's recommended reading list. It's just a bunch of books, and the only thing they have in common is that I bought them, borrowed them, received them as gifts, or had them bequeathed to me by the previous tenants of some of the crummy apartments I've lived in. These books represent neither the best nor the worst of writing. What they do represent is writing that's being published and bought today, writing that's bringing some money and some fame to its authors, writing that works.

Throughout this book, whenever I need an example to make a point I will either write it myself, clip it out of a newspaper or magazine, or cull it from one of those three hundred books. If I lead you to believe that something is an important key to good writing, and then I have to go rummaging through the public library for proof because I can't find a single example out of three hundred miscellaneous published books, then I'm wrong. It's not important.

What About the Games?

Will I be sent directly to hell if I skip the exercises at the ends of chapters? Not necessarily. But the exercises (which I'm calling *games* to make them more inviting) can be fun. If you do them you will get more out of the book. There's no need to write in the book or jot neat columns of numbers. Just grab a pen and some scrap paper and crank up your creativity. Don't feel pressured to get "right" answers. There's no score. The games are not supposed to produce Pulitzer Prize winning prose. They are intended merely to tickle your imagination and help you put into action some of the techniques presented in this book.

These games exist because I found in teaching adult education writing classes that writing lengthy assignments during class is a drag. It makes for a boring evening and lonely students, and since the papers must be written longhand, they're darn near illegible and defy editing. So I give longer assignments as homework, and in class I stick to exercises, like these, that take a minute or two, and then I go around the room and ask each student what he wrote. That way everybody gets the benefit of everyone else's imagination.

Part
TWO
Style

It's Not Just What You Say . . .

A few weeks ago I wanted to learn about the human brain. On one of my exciting trips to the laundromat I stopped at the library and grabbed a couple of brain books off the shelves without browsing through them. A few days later when I found the time to sit back and look at them, I devised a simple test for deciding which book to read. I picked up the first book, flipped to a page at random, and stabbed my finger at it. I landed on this sentence:

But does the greater spontaneity and speed of assimilatory coordination between schemata fully explain the internalisation of behavior, or does representation begin at the present level, thus indicating the transition from sensori-motor intelligence to genuine thought?

Then I grabbed the other brain book, flipped it open, poked in my finger, and landed on this:

If a frog's eyes are rotated 180 degrees, it will move its tongue in the wrong direction for food and will literally starve to death as a result of the inability to compensate for the distortion.

Which book do you think I read?
Which book would you have read?
Both were written by experts on the subject, but unless the reader is also an expert, there is no contest in the fight for reader attention. The second one is just better writing.

The author of the second book used visual images to put what he understands into a form that I understand. I can see that confused little frog's eyes rotating and his tongue shooting off in the wrong direction, while *assimilatory coordination* stuffed into a sentence with *schemata*, *internalisation*, and *sensori-motor intelligence* leaves me more confused than even that frog.

The second author also won me as a reader for the same reason that you will make more friends in Burundi if you brush up on your Swahili. He spoke to me in my language. The expert who wrote the first sentence spoke to me in his own language.

The author's use of visual images and accessible language should establish more firmly in your mind something you already knew when you picked up this book: Style does make a difference. It's not just what you write that matters; it's *how* you write it.

Although too many editors these days emphasize the story, the content, the subject over the technical abilities of the writer, good writers *can* make *any* subject interesting, while incompetent writers can make anything dull.

While you should strive to make all of your writing lively, you should know that you're going to have to work harder at it if your raw material is less than thrilling, such as advertising copy, a sales report, or an essay on time management in the insurance industry. One might even imagine a mathematical formula that says writing that works must be well written in proportion to how dull the subject matter is.

Tomorrow morning you can trot down to your local newsstand and pick up some enormously successful paperbacks that are not particularly well written. However, chances are that they will be about matters intrinsically and universally fascinating, such as the sex lives of last year's Oscar winners.

If, on the other hand, to use a ridiculously unlikely example, someone managed to write a bestselling ode to biology, crammed full of thoughts on such sleep-inducing matters as ant behavior, bacteria, mitochondria, and symbiotic relationships, the style would have to sparkle; it would have to be so clear and sharp that it immediately sliced through the reader's resistance to the subject matter. Impossible? Not at all. Such books, rare though they may be, *are* written and *do* succeed. Outnumbered as they are by their ponderous counterparts, they shine like jewels.

One such rarity was written by Dr. Lewis Thomas, who imagined that people in the street might read about biology if he could put what he understood into language they understood. Thomas wrote *The Lives of a Cell: Notes of a Biology Watcher*, won the National Book Award for it, and sold a lot of copies.

Why? Was it because of his credentials as a scientist? Of course not. There are millions of scientists who will never reach a popular audience. They are good scientists, but they can't write like this:

> Viewed from the distance of the moon, the astonishing thing about the earth, catching the breath, is that it is alive. The photographs show the dry, pounded surface of the moon in the foreground, dead as an old bone. Aloft, floating free beneath the moist, gleaming membrane of bright blue sky, is the rising earth, the only exuberant thing in this part of the cosmos. If you could look long enough, you would see the swirling of the great drifts of white cloud, covering and uncovering the half-hidden masses of land. If you had been looking for a very long, geologic time, you could have seen the continents themselves in motion, drifting apart on their crustal plates, held afloat by the fire beneath. It has the organized, self-contained look of a live creature, full of information, marvelously skilled in handling the sun.

Yes, the story is important; the subject matter is the big draw. But it will help immensely if you can learn to write of the "dry, pounded surface" that is "dead as an old bone," the "gleaming membrane of bright blue sky," and the "crustal plates, held afloat by the fire beneath." Thomas's book didn't sell because of what he wrote about, but because of *how* he wrote about it.

I work a couple of days a week as assistant managing editor of the *UU World*, which you probably never heard of unless you happen to be a Unitarian Universalist. One of my functions in that job is to receive a lot of dreadfully written material about great Unitarian or Universalist historical figures, people like Michael Servetus, Origen, and Francis David. The information I get about these people arrives in the form of church-anniversary brochures, sermons that someone thinks will make good editorials, or short histories written for no apparent reason.

These treatises on the giants of liberal religion are not only of scant interest to the general public, they seem carefully crafted to lull even a dedicated Unitarian Universalist into a state of catatonia. Recently I realized that I had come to think of Servetus, David, and their cohorts as dull, when in reality they were colorful, exciting men who had the misfortune to be chronicled in words not wisely chosen.

I was cured of this misconception recently when a booklet called *400 Years* showed up on my desk. Yet another history of Francis David and King John Sigismund, this one is nineteen pages long, and was issued by the First Unitarian Society of Minneapolis. I'm sure I must have groaned, and braced myself for boredom when I picked it up, knowing I would have to read at least three pages before I could in good conscience throw it away. But this one was different. The project had been put in the hands of someone who could write. His name is Edward Darling, and his booklet begins:

> During the dark and bloody days of the Emperor Charles V and the vicious, tooth and claw free-for-all between the Holy Roman Empire and the Sultan for the control of eastern Europe, there developed in Transylvania a true-life drama the like of which the world had never seen. It was an almost incredible happening which is still regarded by scholars as a miracle of history. And it was played out on a stage wide enough to include Buba and Constantinople—although the central action was in the Land Beyond the Forest—Transylvania.

Of course I read on. Wouldn't you? Material I had always resisted now attracted me. How had Edward Darling captured me as a reader?

I read Darling's *400 Years* for the same reason I read the brain book by the author who wrote of the frog that moved its tongue in the wrong direction, for the same reason I read Lewis Thomas's *Lives of a Cell*. Each of these writers presented material I could have gotten a dozen other places.

There was nothing unique about the substance of their work, but "the way in which something is said or done as distinguished from its substance" made all the difference. (That's my dictionary's definition of *style*.) They had all captured me with their style.

As you read books about writing and take writing classes, you will find that *style* is one of those writing terms that never seems to mean the same thing twice. You cannot corral it into one neat definition any more than you can stuff a cloud into a burlap bag. It's vague. It's fluid. It wriggles when you try to grab it.

When I began to outline this section, I came to the disconcerting conclusion that half of everything I wanted to say in this book could legitimately be deposited in a chapter on Style. Some jerk could even come along and nail me good with the argument that *all* writing instruction is about style, because style is the *way* a thing is said, not *what* is said. All writing can be viewed as style because, even though there are other aspects to writing (such as description, dialogue, and characterization), words or phrases can be many different things at one time, depending on how you look at them. This section of the book is about one way of looking at them, a way that is called *style*.

Now that we have a few thousand years of written language behind us, we've begun to notice that some stuff gets read and some stuff gets tossed directly into the wastebasket. If we study enough of both kinds, we begin to see some common denominators; we observe how some words in certain combinations can hold readers and how some turn them off. In other words, writing that works and writing that doesn't work. These observations, especially when applied to writing in general, are called *rules of style*. In a sense, *every* statement one makes about good writing is a rule of style, and I could make them up all night long. But I won't. I'll stick to the important ones.

Eschew Verbosity

Sooner or later in your writing career, a teacher or an editor will return a manuscript with the notation "too wordy."

Wordiness, as generally used by teachers, editors, and writers, has two possible meanings. One is the second definition in my dictionary: "Expressed in or using more words than are necessary to convey meaning." We'll get to that soon.

The other way you can be guilty of wordiness is by using long words when short ones will do, using rare words instead of common ones, using words that look as if they were erected instead of written.

Such wordiness occurs in the example I gave you earlier from my short-lived novel, *The Rabbit Knows*:

So he stood torpidly on the pebbled border of the lifeless highway with his arm outstretched across the corroded asphalt and his thumb sought some sort of concession to his distress, and once again he found himself making nugatory conjectures.

Do you know what *torpidly* means? Do you know what *nugatory conjectures* are?

I don't, and I wrote that mess.

This sort of wordiness can put your reader to sleep as fast as the wordiness in that sentence I came upon in the first brain book:

"But does the greater spontaneity and speed of assimilatory

coordination between schemata fully . . . '' zzz.

Generally speaking, words like these, especially when used frequently, just don't work.

By ''words like these'' I mean words that are unfamiliar to most of your readers, words that reduce or eliminate the reader's comprehension of a sentence. I also mean words with which the reader is familiar but not intimate, words that add complexity to an idea without returning something in precision or color.

These words don't work because no matter how specific and accurate a word is, it is worthless if your reader doesn't know what it means. In fact, it is worse than worthless, because it might turn your reader away from your writing.

These words don't work because they interrupt the reader with the question ''What does that mean?'' They create an unexpected noise in his head and remind him that there is a writer at work just as surely as the shattering of glass and the shrieking of an alarm tell him there is a burglar at work.

This sort of wordiness generally results from insecurity, the need to impress people with your vocabulary, and the fear that if you write ''the guy on the horse'' they'll think you didn't know the word *equestrian*. I speak from experience, believe me: I'm *still* embarrassed when I read some of my old stories, nugatory conjectures and all.

This sort of wordiness also results from an overdependence on the thesaurus. The thesaurus is a book of synonyms. It's a very valuable tool for a writer. Get one, but don't use it to look up a lot of words you've never seen before. Use it to look up words that are colorful and precise and mean exactly what you want to say. You know thousands of such words, but they don't always rise to the surface of your brain.

Obviously you will use many words that are unfamiliar to some of your readers. If you tried to stick to words that every single reader understood, you would end up writing about Dick and Jane and Spot.

But, of each word you use, ask these questions:

Have most of my readers seen and understood this word many times before?

Will the readers who don't know the word lose the meaning of the sentence, or will the context clear it up for them and possibly give them a new word?

If they have to look it up in the dictionary, is this the only time they'll need to, or will they spend more time with Webster's book than with mine?

So use simple words. But don't confuse simple with dull. Words are rarely dull by themselves, but, like recollections of birdies on the sixteenth hole, they become dull when you hear them over and over. So when repetition threatens to bore your reader, draw on that treasury of *simple but interesting* words. If *walk* is dull, *stroll* is simple but interesting, and *perambulate* is wordy. If talk is getting wearisome, then have people chat, bicker, or shoot the breeze, but don't let them discourse or expatiate, except on rare occasions. If too many people are getting wet in the rain, have a few get soaked or drenched, but please don't let anyone become moisture-laden.

Remember: *Writing gets more interesting as it acquires precision, not length.*

A Wordiness Game

Make a list of ten common words that can become dull through repetition (such as *man*, *book*, *sat*). For each word try to come up with a synonym that is simple but interesting and a synonym that is wordy. (You may have to hunt through the thesaurus, but don't for a minute entertain the idea that that's "cheating." The writing profession has tools, just as any other does, and you wouldn't think a carpenter was cheating because he used his saw.)

After you've compiled your lists, put the words into sentences. Lock yourself alone in a quiet room. Sit and relax and get yourself into a meditative state. Read your sentences aloud, and try to get in touch with the subtle effects that words have on your brain, your concentration. We'll talk more about this at length later, but for now just try to feel that split second of apathy that comes when you read a dull word, the apathy that makes you close a book when it occurs again and again. Try to feel that fleeting rush of enthusiasm that comes when you see that someone *sprinted* or people *bickered*. The simple but interesting words are what draw you into a piece of writing and keep you there. Finally, try to feel the subtle tension in your body, the annoyance, the almost imperceptible anger you experience when your reading is interrupted by a noisy stranger like *perambulated*, *expatiated*, or *torpidly*.

Ultimately, nobody can give you a list of good words and bad words, words that are familiar to your reader and words that are not. Sometimes there are even good reasons to write about nugatory conjectures and moisture-laden objects. We'll talk about some of them later. But if you read enough, and write enough, and listen to enough conversations, you will develop an ear for words that work and words that don't.

The other definition of wordiness is concerned not with the quality of words, but with the quantity. Many new writers use too many words too often, and all writers use too many words sometimes.

You don't put extra words into a sentence for the same reason you don't tape two toilet brushes to the windshield of your car: they wouldn't serve any purpose, and they would get in the way.

The reason fewer words is better will be clear to you if you can remember walking through the schoolyard and having some smart-aleck kid say, "Hey, which is heavier, a pound of feathers or a pound of iron?" and after you cleverly figured out that they both weighed the same, he said, "Oh yeah? Then which would you rather have dropped on your head?"

The reason iron would be your second choice, though it weighed the same as the feathers, is density. Iron has more weight per square inch. It has more *impact*.

So it is with words. The smaller the number of words you use to contain a thought or an image, the more *impact* that thought or image will have.

Consider the impact of this six-word classified ad:

"For sale: Baby's crib. Never used."

The overemployment of words generally takes three forms: redundant words, wasted words, and weak words.

Redundant words. The dictionary says redundant means "needlessly repetitive," which has led people who are feeling witty to say things like "It's redundant to commit suicide in Kansas," or " 'Boring insurance salesman' is a redundant phrase."

Redundancy occurs when you use two or more words to say something that is already being said clearly by one of them. "Baby puppies" is redundant. A "little midget" would be redundant, as would a "big giant," a "long-necked giraffe," or "six a.m. in the morning." "Red in color" is redundant because a thing can't be red in size, shape, or age. Try to find the redundant phrases in your own work and the work of others. (One way to enjoy commercials is to listen for the redundant phrases. This morning I heard a commercial for a product that promised "long-lasting durability.")

Redundancy doesn't always come in neat little two- or three-word phrases, though. Often you will find two words doing the same job in separate parts of a sentence:

"Lenore picked up a weekly paycheck every Friday." (If it happens every Friday, then we know it's weekly.)

"Immortalized in stone, he would live forever."

Wasted words. When you write, don't use extra words that serve no purpose; they slow your writing down. Wasted words frequently show up in the form of overused, meaningless phrases like "in the event of" (if); "on the occasion of" (when); "owing to the fact that" (because); "for a period of a month" (for a month).

Words are also wasted in an attempt to modify that which cannot be modified, as in "*very* unique" and "*slightly* impossible." These phrases seem to be the special pets of the educated but insecure, those people who think that more words equals more thought and knowledge. Wasted words proliferate in business memos, government manuals, Rotary Club speeches, grant proposals, even pay-by-the-word want ads.

Weak words. One of the best ways to improve what you have written is to throw out two or three weak words and replace them with a strong one that conveys the same meaning. Listen to what happens when:

"Lee was a mean woman" becomes "Lee was a shrew."

"He was a generous and thoughtful man" becomes "He was a saint."

"He passed away early in the morning, and people all over America cried" becomes "He died at dawn and the nation wept."

When you can change ten words to seven, or two words to one, the writing almost always will work better.

Here's a tip for finding weak words. Be wary of adverbs ending in *-ly*, such as *rapidly, perversely,* and *lavishly*. They often pop up because you used a weak verb and tried to boost it. Whenever possible, chuck them in the wastebasket and replace them with stronger verbs.

For example, if Stan *jumped suddenly* upon the burglar, your reader will see it better if you say he *pounced* upon the burglar. If Maria *ate* her supper *quickly* in order to keep her date with Mark, your reader will see it better if Maria *gobbled* her supper.

(Note, particularly in the second example, how the stronger verb gives your reader not only a clearer picture of the specific action, but also a stronger sense of the overall mood and the emotions involved.)

An "-ly" Game

Change these weak verbs with adverbs into strong, colorful verbs that have more *impact*.

1. Spoke boringly.
2. Smiled happily.
3. Wrote nervously.
4. Hit angrily.
5. Looked curiously.
6. Touched affectionately.
7. Departed quickly.

Pruning your prose is not a chore. It's as much fun as any word game. When you spot the redundancy or weed out the wasted words or come up with a stronger verb, you feel clever. You feel like a writer.

However, don't become a fanatic about it. Don't cross out every word you could possibly do without. Just be sure that every word you use has a job to do.

If the word is doing some work, such as providing needed information, creating a clearer picture, or reminding the reader of something important, then let it stay. But if it's lazy, not earning its keep, throw it out.

There is no perfection to be attained in any of this. Just as you can never pull all the weeds from a garden, you will never eliminate all the useless words from your writing. You can pick up any book or magazine in the world and find words that are just not working. As I glance over these last few pages, I see that I wrote "windshield of your car," "they both weighed the same," and "the special pets."

Oh well. The war on wordiness continues.

Use Active Voice . . . Most of the Time

A guy I know hangs around his apartment every evening in front of the television, hoping somebody will call and invite him to dinner. In the afternoon he haunts the mailbox, figuring maybe an invitation or a check will show up from some unexpected source. He dreams about new friends coming into his life, a better job popping up out of nowhere, and he figures he might win a new car someday if a disc jockey calls him up and asks an easy question.

I know another fellow who plays tennis every morning. When he meets a man or a woman he'd like to know better, he gets the phone number and calls the person up. This guy started his own business a few years back, and now he's putting the profits into businesses started by his friends. He also likes to go skydiving.

Which man do you find more interesting, the passive one who lets things happen to him, or the active one who makes things happen?

The active man is more interesting. In writing, too, active is more interesting than passive. Just as you would fix your attention on the active man and ignore the passive one, your reader will fix his attention on the active words and phrases.

New writers often fall into the habit of casting their characters as the passive recipients of some activity, when they should be writing about people or objects doing things, making things happen.

Compare "The marks given to me were exceptional" with "I got all A's"; "The symptoms of a cold were felt by Nora all night" with "Nora coughed, wheezed, and sniffled all night."

Write about people, not things, whenever possible. That is often the key to finding the interesting active voice. For example, "A good time was had by all" should be purged from every church newsletter in the world. It's a passive sentence about "good times" when it should be about people.

"Everybody had a good time" is an active sentence about people. The Sunday schoolers had a good time. The Ladies Aid had a good time. The visiting bishop had a good time.

Sometimes, however, you are not writing about people, but about objects or concepts. Even then your objects or concepts should take charge of the sentence, become the subject, and work in the active voice.

For example, "The car was driven by Morty." If you're writing about Morty, then "Morty drove the car." But maybe you're really writing about the car. In that case, "The car sped down the highway," "took over the interstate," "swung around curves," or "crashed into a fruit stand." In other words, the car *did* something.

The tip-off to these dull, passive-voice sentences is usually a compound verb like *was driven* or *were presented*. Cash them in for sharp, short, interesting, active verbs, and your writing will work better.

An "Active Voice" Game

See if you can make these sentences as interesting as that man who plays tennis and goes skydiving by putting them into the active voice.

1. Ninety-four strikes were bowled by the team from Manny's Cafe.
2. The atomic bomb was first dropped by the Americans.
3. Three rings came from the telephone during the night.

4. Nine runs were scored by the Toronto Blue Jays in the fifth inning.
5. The tree was struck by a bolt of lightning.
6. A speech was given by President Lincoln in Gettysburg.

Be Specific . . . Most of the Time

Through the window by my desk I can look down on Blossom Lane. (No kidding. That's really the name of the street I live on.) Right now there is a man down there wearing clothes of all different colors. They are bright, but mismatched.

Can you see him?

His shirt is blue. His pants are yellow. His shoes are brown. His jacket is fire-engine red. And he's wearing a green fedora.

Can you see him better now?

One objective you will find in the *be specific* rule, and throughout this book, is to make your writing more visual. If you can show your reader a clear, well-focused image, something he can really see, you will hold his interest. Do you remember that frog whose eyes had been rotated 180 degrees?

Being specific is one way you can draw clearer pictures.

I know a girl who was attacked by a dog yesterday. I know another girl who was attacked by a Doberman pinscher. Which dog can you see more clearly—the vague, general dog, or the specific dog? Which attack is more believable?

Which can you see better—a gun, or a Smith & Wesson .38? A car, or a red Corvette? A woman, or a nun?

As I get more specific, I bring the picture into clearer focus. For the reader, seeing is believing.

Like all of these rules, *be specific* is a generalization. You should look for the vague areas in your writing and try to improve them by zeroing in. But don't be specific just for the hell of it.

I'll give you a couple of examples of how being specific for its own sake could make your writing worse, not better.

In the case of the dog attacking the girl, I could say the dog was a black Doberman pinscher with a broken chain dangling from his neck, blood on his teeth, one ear missing from a previous fight, and the letter *L* carved on his rump. All of this would etch a picture of the dog more deeply on the reader's imagination. This would be great if I were writing a description for the policeman who's got to hunt the dog down. But assuming this is a story or a newspaper report, the more I belabor the dog, the more it becomes what the passage is about, and I'm really trying to tell you about an attack, not a dog. So, instead of going on and on about this angry beast, I try to create a sharply focused image with one or two specific words such as *vicious* or *enraged*.

Here is another way I could misuse the *be specific* rule.

Let's say my sentence is "Still alone with her fears, Jennifer rose from the table, coffee cup in hand, and gazed out the kitchen window."

Now a window is a fairly general kind of thing, and I could show it to you much better by saying it was a stained-glass window, or a three-inch window, or a window made out of old pickle jars. All of those things make the window more specific.

Unfortunately, they also make the window a freak, because windows are all pretty much the same. Unlike a dog, one window usually looks very much like another. Stained-glass windows, tiny windows, and windows that have little chipmunks painted on them all clash with the reader's expectations. You weren't shocked to find out that the dog that attacked a girl was a Doberman, but you were probably so taken aback when you entered Jennifer's otherwise ordinary kitchen for the first time and found eighty-two pickle jars for a window that you probably forgot all about "her fears," which were supposed to be the important thing.

So *be specific* with items that come in a well-known variety of shapes, colors, textures, and sizes, but don't put any weird windows in your stories and articles unless they do something important.

A "Be Specific" Game

Here are five sentences containing common general nouns:

1. The car became worthless within hours of its purchase.
2. The man only had one arm.
3. He handed her the book before he said goodbye.
4. She stood on the chair to reach the lightbulb.
5. It was Christmas morning, and only one toy sat beneath the tree.

Try to make the sentences more vivid by adding adjectives that make the nouns more specific. For example, the small tragedy "Sam drove in too quickly and crushed his daughter's toy" becomes a bit more poignant when you say "Sam drove in too quickly and crushed his daughter's new toy." New toys and old toys are both easier to see than toys.

And you could make the embarrassing incident "Kate tried to slip quietly out of the crowded auditorium, but knocked over the chair as she rose" just a little more embarrassing by writing "Kate tried to slip quietly out of the crowded auditorium, but knocked over the metal chair as she rose."

Which can you see and hear better, a chair being knocked over or a metal chair being knocked over?

(Note also that you can see this little incident better because it's not just in an auditorium; it's in a *crowded* auditorium.)

Now make another list of five nouns. Instead of making them more specific by adding an adjective, make them more specific by changing the noun, just as I changed dog to Doberman.

For example, change "She married a rich man who walked with a limp" to "She married a rich Mexican who walked with a limp."

Two tips about being specific:

Tip #1: *Being specific is particularly useful in creating humor.*

My wife Nora goes to art school, and she says her oil painting class had a laughing fit last week when one of the women in the class cried "Oh, my God," and someone asked "What's the matter?" and the woman said "I just sat in my Thalo Green."

If she had said "I just sat in my paint," it wouldn't have been good for more than a chuckle.

Tip #2: *Being specific with numbers increases believability.*

Which can you see better, "Some thugs jumped him as he came out of the liquor store" or "Six thugs jumped him as he came out of the liquor store"?

The exact number is more believable because it sounds as if you were there to count them.

Say Things in a Positive Way . . . Most of the Time

Writing about what is or was true usually creates a clearer, more interesting picture than writing about what isn't or wasn't true. It works better. (This is another generalization. Practice it, but don't become obsessed with it.)

Which can you see better, "He was not a generous man" or "He was a miser"?

"The painting did not have any flaws" or "It was a masterpiece"?

"He did not treat his kids nicely" or "He brutalized his children"?

"She did not write interesting sermons" or "Her sermons put parishioners to sleep"?

"Phil was not a graceful person" or "Phil was a klutz"?

Tell the reader the truth. Be straightforward. Show him what you want to show him, not what you don't want him to see.

If you tell a reader there is no light in a room, the first thing he's going to see is the light that's not there. Tell him the room is dark, and he'll see darkness.

A "Say Things in a Positive Way" Game

Make these negative sentences more interesting by putting them in a positive form:

1. The smell that permeated the room was not pleasant.
2. By five o'clock there were no tickets left for the Knicks-Lakers game.
3. Several publishers told Ms. Spencer they didn't want her manuscript.
4. There had not been a dry day all week.
5. President Carter did not hold the news conference that was scheduled for Thursday.

Show, Don't Tell
. . . Most of the Time

"Marilyn French smiles a lot when she speaks to you, and often she chuckles. She's not as angry as her book would have you believe, but she *is* angry, and sometimes when she's sitting on the couch, smiling, she can express that anger in a very cold fashion."

There is nothing wrong with that passage. It's grammatically correct, it's clear, and it provides information. But if I wrote a whole book or an article that way, you probably would not survive to the end. The paragraph *tells* you that Marilyn French chuckles. It *tells* you that she's angry. It *tells* you that she sits on the couch, smiles, expresses anger.

The problem is that all readers are from Missouri: They want to be shown. As much as possible, *show, don't tell* your readers what you want them to see.

Instead of *telling* my readers the above information in a *Writer's Yearbook* profile of Marilyn French, I wanted to *show* them. Read what happened.

Marilyn French smiles a lot when she speaks to you, and such statements can rise from her on the crest of a chuckle. Unlike her book, she does not pulsate with anger. But the anger is there—big jagged chunks of it careening through her body to be tossed out when she needs them—and sometimes even as the trace of a smile hangs on her face and her soft round body is coiled like a kitten's on the couch, she can say what she needs to say with all the cold efficiency of a highly paid assassin.

Show, don't tell.

Show means create a picture the reader can see.

If you do an interview with Larry Bird for *Sports Illustrated*, you can *tell* your reader "Larry Bird is a very tall man," or you can *show* him: "Bird ducked as he came through the doorway to the living room."

Can you see his height better?

You can tell your reader the girl in your story "had bright blue eyes," or you can show him: "Her eyes sparkled like distant lakes in the sunshine."

I know a guy who is cruel. And I know another guy who whips his horse.

Whose cruelty repels you more? Who can you see better? Which man, though cruel, is more interesting?

The key words here, as in most writing, are the verbs. I made the writing work better by turning adjectives that tell into verbs that show. I turned the adjective *tall* into the verb *ducked*. I turned the adjective *bright* into the verb *sparkled*. I turned the adjective *cruel* into the verb *whips*. Verbs work better than adjectives.

Look for the adjectives that tell, and try to turn them into verbs that show. Ask yourself this question: What would he, she, or it *do* because he, she, or it has this quality?

A man cries because he has sadness. A girl crouches because she has fear. A plane roars because it has loudness.

A "Show, Don't Tell" Game

Make a list of five nouns preceded by adjectives that tell. Try to turn the adjectives into verbs that show. For example, if your list were loud man, happy dog, old paint, shiny coin, and sad woman, you might come up with: man roared, dog wagged tail, paint peeled, coin glinted, and woman wept.

Try these just to get your brain in gear.

1. Embarrassed girl
2. Impatient trucker
3. Angry coach
4. Despondent widower
5. Reluctant student
6. Overheated engine
7. Nervous elephant
8. Drunken minister

☛ ☛ ☛ ☛ ☛ ☛ ☛   **Coffee Break**

There's a McDonald's about half a mile from my place, and once or twice a week I go there to sort out all the threads of my writing career. As a freelance writer I always have several projects going at once, and when my brain gets crowded and needs to be emptied, I need someplace that is symbolically away from it all.

I go to McDonald's not for the gourmet food, but because I

can have a table to myself without being waited on or charged a minimum. I get a cup of coffee and sit for an hour or more scribbling with a blue ballpoint pen into a hardbacked lined notebook. This "McDonald's fix" is invariably a productive period. I come up with leads for articles, discover visual ways of presenting the abstract, make lists of characters, and just generally get my head reorganized for writing.

There's no particular reason why you should go to McDonald's, write with a blue ballpoint pen, or use a hardbacked pad of paper. But I think it helps to have a special place, pen, and paper as cues for the sense of being away from it while still dealing with it. A writer needs from time to time to get away from his regular writing place, to be alone with himself, to view his work from a distance.

If you've just read the last six rules of style in one sitting, you've probably got what I call "glut brain," a head crowded with information and the need to articulate it. So it might be a good time for you to grab a pen and a notebook, pour a cup of coffee, and sit someplace where you don't ordinarily sit. Start by scribbling down what you remember, but go on and add to it, improve it, invent your own examples and observations. Tell yourself what you know, and then prove to yourself you know it by elaborating.

Before you do that, however, I want to give you just one more thing to think about.

As you read these rules of style, you may think you hear many things repeated. That's because the rules overlap. They dovetail. Tickle one and another giggles. When you follow the rule to *be specific* or *use active voice*, you often eliminate words, so you *avoid wordiness*. When you *show, don't tell*, you often turn a passive sentence into an active one.

Writing that works in one sense is usually writing that works in another.

Appeal to the Senses

Through the senses of sight, sound, taste, smell, and touch we reach out to the world; we experience. We perceive life with these senses, and our memories are the memories of those perceptions. Writing that works is writing that appeals to the senses. So always in your writing return to the senses. The abstracts you create, the "think" material, float tenuously on the surface of the brain and can be blown away by the ringing of the telephone. But when you appeal to the reader's senses, you give him something to latch on to, an image that can be re-created with the mention of a single word. Sight. Sound. Taste. Smell. Touch. Through these channels you will most effectively reach your reader.

I've talked about the sense of sight in writing. (Show, don't tell. Remember that frog.) Sight is the sense we use most. Even in sleep we use the *sense* of sight to perceive our dreams. But the worlds you want to bring alive with your writing are also rich in other sensory stimuli, the sounds, the smells, the flavors, and the peculiar tactile sensations that come from textures and temperature and motion.

While you can't load every paragraph you write with sights, sounds, and smells, you should return again and again to the senses to remind the reader that this written world is the same one he lives in. It sparkles, it roars, it rubs against him, and sometimes it stinks.

You will find that appealing to the senses works especially well at the beginning of an article or story, when you are leading the reader into your written world. "See," you are saying, "it's made of the same stuff as the world you're in now."

Here is the lead for an article I did on carnivals. See how many words you can find that appeal directly to the senses.

It is a world that leaves its imprint on your senses for a lifetime.

Years later you catch the smell of strawberries and you can remember nipping at big curls of cotton candy piled high on a paper cone. Or on a dry day and a dusty road when clouds of fine brown dust swirl around your feet, you recall a stroll down the midway, her hand clasped in yours, and you wonder what ever became of her. One early morning the fragrance of freshly cut grass rushes to meet you and you are immediately transported back to that tentative summer world of your childhood.

It is of course the summer carnival, a chimerical, warm-weather vision that rises from a vacant lot one sultry night and greets you in the morning. It has been stirring the imaginations of children and the memories of adults for hundreds of years.

The memories it stirs are romantic for some, adventurous for others. But whether you celebrate the courage it took to climb onto that towering Ferris wheel for the first time or the courage it took years later to call up a girl and ask her to go to the carnival with you, it seems that the carnival itself is as much a part of growing up as a taste of beer and the high school dance.

Of course, not all carnival memories are fond ones. It is, after all, a place where huge clanking machines fling you in circles, and if you are prone to nausea your condition is only worsened by the ubiquitous fumes of diesel engines, the blare of rock music, and the three hot dogs you devoured much too quickly.

If you interview the governor of Kentucky or a woman who raises ducks, and you want to make your subject real to the reader, consider how you might move through those highly accessible channels, the senses, to bring the person right into the room with the reader.

Did the governor get embarrassed? Or did his face turn red,

did his fingers tremble slightly, did moisture rise to the surface of his palms?

Does the duck woman smoke a lot? Or does she have two fingers that are as brown as fresh-baked bread from nicotine stains; does the air in her office reek with the smoke rising from half a dozen ashtrays?

Think about your subject in a sensory way. Sure, he's a nice guy, he's dynamic, he has accomplished a great deal. But what of the senses? When you shook his hand was it warm or cool, wet or dry? Is he shaped like a tree or a pillow? What sort of sounds does he make? Is his voice harsh? Can you hear his footsteps?

The senses are touchstones for the reader. Return to them often. They work.

In the game we're going to play next, I'll ask you to find things that appeal to all five senses within different environments. It's good practice. But in most of your writing, you'll be working mainly with three senses: sight, sound, and touch. Except for eating, drinking, smoking, and kissing, we don't associate taste with most experiences, and if you tried to find a taste or flavor for each experience you wrote about, your writing would not work. The same goes for the sense of smell. Thousands of objects emit a smell, but we usually only think about the stronger smells, such as the scents of flowers, the aromas of food, and the gagging stenches of cigarette smoke and bus exhaust. A specific smell used in the right place can work wonders in making your writing work for the reader. Proust, for example, did a lot with very subtle fragrances—limeflower tea, etc. But go easy. Too many writers load their prose with every olfactory sensation they can imagine, everything from the pungency of aging pickles to the aroma of freshly picked cotton.

An "Appeal to the Senses" Game

Think about these five environments:

1. A circus

2. A high school gymnasium
3. A fisherman's wharf
4. An auto-racing track
5. A neighborhood bar

For each place write a paragraph or several sentences, using all five senses to describe the environment.

For example, if your environment were a "movie theater," you might mention the sight of an usher, the sound of some bratty kid kicking the back of a seat, the smell of popcorn, the taste of a candy bar, and the feel of the floor that is invariably sticky from spilled sodas and discarded wads of chewing gum.

The important thing to remember is that you should use sensory stimuli that are associated with that environment but not with environments in general. If you say "It was noisy at the baseball game," you haven't gained any ground in trying to engrave the image of a baseball game on the reader's brain. But if the noises you mention are the crack of the bat, the whizzing of a fastball, the roar of the crowd, the heckling from the bleachers, and the hush that falls over the stadium when one more strike will complete a no-hitter, then you have used "baseball words" to remind the reader of where he is.

Weigh Jargon Carefully

Writing for publication is not the same as taking an English exam. In the former you're trying to make the writing work for the reader. In the latter you're trying to please the teacher so you'll get an A.

In making your decisions to use marginal words or to use them in questionable ways, don't ask yourself if your high school English teacher would approve. Ask yourself "Would it make the writing work? Would it help to etch the image I want on the reader's brain?"

If you try to keep track of all the words that are jargon, slang, or colloquial, all the words that are "unacceptable" or "improper usage," and edit them from your work, I can promise you you'll turn into a raving lunatic and you'll be locked up in a state hospital where you'll spend the rest of your life howling through the bars on your window, *"Contact* is not a verb. *Like* is not a conjunction. *Upscale* doesn't mean anything."

We do need consistent rules of usage. We also need to forbid some words entry into our language. Words and the forms they take must be consistent in order to be recognizable. If a word means something different every time you see it, it has no meaning at all.

It's true that the indiscriminate acceptance of new words could ruin our language and reduce it to a general shorthand lacking both nuance and beauty. It's true that jargon, particularly when it originates on Madison Avenue, can scrape your nerves and triple your pulse rate as it's jammed down your eustachian tubes by people who have buckets of cash to pay for moronic TV commericals and vulgar billboards.

But it's also true that our language is rich with words that were once considered unacceptable, words that were once shunned and scorned, but are now employed to say what no other words can say. They've earned their way into our language.

I think the problem is that many teachers, editors, and writers approach the issue of jargon and slang not in a practical way, but as a moral crusade. They see new words as Huns swooping down from the hills to rape our mother tongue.

But even these vigilantes don't always agree on just who the bad guys are. Language laws cannot be enforced. There are too many opinions, disagreements, and special cases. If you try to always be "right," you'll end up crazy instead.

My advice is that you look at words of dubious reputation not as interlopers or criminals, but as job applicants. They want to join the language. They want to be part of your writing. So ask yourself if they work. Are they worth the space they occupy? Will they do the job they are hired for? Listen to them carefully. How do they land upon the ear? Give them a trial period. If they work well, keep them. If they don't, you know what to do. Of course, you should maintain high standards. Don't latch on to every new word that comes down the pike, just as you wouldn't hire every bozo who drifted into the personnel office. But listen to each word. Give it a chance.

For me there are words that just don't work. My friend Jan called recently to tell me she'd been named as "facilitator" for some group or other. I immediately lost interest. Then there are the people who are always "orientating" themselves, which sounds to me as if they are getting oriented while rotating.

On the other hand, if some girl grabbed the money and "split," I can see her fleeing, and if a man tells me his divorce trial was a real "bummer," I know exactly what he means. These words work for me, so I expect them to work in my writing.

A Personal Writing Style?

Your personal writing style is what makes your description of a one-legged gnu different from mine. Since we both have the goal of showing the reader a one-legged gnu, the different ways we do it won't be crucial, assuming we both understand the basics of writing that works.

There are some writers, however, who develop a style as specific as their thumbprints. The writing of journalist Tom Wolfe, for example, can be spotted without a byline. Anyone familiar with Wolfe's work would quickly recognize this passage from "Las Vegas (What?) Las Vegas (Can't hear you! Too noisy) Las Vegas! !!!", which appeared in *The Kandy-Kolored Tangerine-Flake Streamline Baby* (Farrar, Straus & Giroux,

1965), as Wolfe's or the work of a clever imitator.

Hernia, hernia, hernia, hernia, hernia, hernia, hernia, hernia, hernia, hernia, hernia, hernia, hernia, HERNia; hernia, HERNia, hernia, hernia, hernia, hernia, HERNia, HERNia, HERNia; hernia, hernia, hernia, hernia, hernia, hernia, hernia, eight is the point, the point is eight; hernia, hernia, HERNia; hernia, hernia, hernia, hernia, all right, hernia, hernia, hernia, hernia, hard eight, hernia, hernia, hernia, HERNia, hernia, hernia, hernia, HERNia, hernia, hernia, hernia, HERNia, hernia, hernia, hernia, hernia

"What is all this *hernia hernia* stuff?"

This was Raymond talking to the wavy-haired fellow with the stick, the dealer, at the craps table about 3:45 Sunday morning. The stickman had no idea what this big wiseacre was talking about, but he resented the tone. He gave Raymond that patient arch of the eyebrows known as a Red Hook brushoff, which is supposed to convey some such thought as, I am a very tough but cool guy, as you can tell by the way I carry my eyeballs low in the pouches, and if this wasn't such a high-class joint we would take wiseacres like you out back and beat you into jellied madrilene.

At this point, however, Raymond was immune to subtle looks.

The stickman tried to get the game going again, but every time he would start up his singsong, by easing the words out through the nose, which seems to be the style among craps dealers in Las Vegas—"All right, a new shooter . . . eight is the point, the point is eight" and so on—Raymond would start droning along with him in exactly the same tone of voice, "Hernia, hernia, hernia; hernia, HERNia, HERNia, hernia; hernia, hernia, hernia."

Everybody at the craps table was staring in consternation to think that anybody would try to needle a tough, hip, elite *soldat* like a Las Vegas craps dealer. The gold-lame odalisques of Los Angeles were staring. The Western sports, fifty-eight-year-old men who wear Texas string ties, were staring. The old babes at the slot machines, holding Dixie Cups full of nickles, were staring at the craps tables, but cranking away the whole time.

Hunter S. Thompson is another contemporary journalist whose style is like a signature on every subject he touches. For this he gets the benefit of loyal fans who flock to him for something they can't get elsewhere. (On the other hand, he might be writing himself into a corner, because his style consists of a very subjective view, reams of exaggeration, flights of fancy, and outright fiction in the midst of fact, which turns a lot of people off.)

This passage from Thompson's *Fear and Loathing in Las Vegas* (Random House, 1971) shows his approach to the same city.

A week in Vegas is like stumbling into a Time Warp, a regression to the late fifties. Which is wholly understandable when you see the people who come here, the Big Spenders from places like Denver and Dallas. Along with National Elks Club conventions (no niggers allowed) and the All-West Volunteer Sheepherders' Rally. These are people who go absolutely crazy at the sight of an old hooker stripping down to her pasties and prancing out on the runway to the big-beat sound of a dozen 50-year-old junkies kicking out the jams on "September Song."

It was some time around three when we pulled into the parking lot of the North Vegas diner. I was looking for a copy of the Los Angeles *Times*, for news of the outside world, but a quick glance at the newspaper racks made a bad joke of that notion. They don't need the *Times* in North Vegas. No news is good news.

"Fuck newspapers," said my attorney. "What we need right now is coffee."

I agreed, but I stole a copy of the Vegas *Sun* anyway. It was yesterday's edition, but I didn't care. The idea of entering a coffee shop without a newspaper in my hands made me nervous. There was always the Sports Section; get wired on the baseball scores and pro-football rumors: "Bart Starr Beaten by Thugs in Chicago Tavern; Packers Seek Trade" . . . "Namath Quits Jets to be Governor of Alabama" . . . and a speculative piece on page 46 about a rookie sensation named Harrison Fire, out of Grambling: runs the hundred in nine flat, 344 pounds and still growing.

"This man Fire has definite promise," says the coach. "Yesterday, before practice, he destroyed a Greyhound Bus with his bare hands, and last night he killed a subway. He's a natural for color TV. I'm not one to play favorites, but it looks like we'll have to make room for him."

Indeed. There is always room on TV for a man who can beat people to jelly in nine flat . . . But not many of these were gathered, on this night, in the North Star Coffee Lounge. We had the place to ourselves—which proved to be fortunate, because we'd eaten two more pellets of mescaline on the way over, and the effects were beginning to manifest.

Don't worry about your personal writing style. It's not something that Tom Wolfe has and you lack; it's just that his is more distinctive. In time you will fall into writing patterns, you'll develop a habit of doing it this way more often than that way. You don't have to consciously cultivate a style. Just learn to write well, and your style will emerge.

No doubt there is a moron somewhere typing up his theory of "writing style analysis," which says that if you use a lot of short sentences you can plan on dying young, and if you're stingy with the commas you're probably a Pisces. Well, maybe. But it's best not to get analytical about your writing style. Just as you cannot acquire peace while yearning for peace, you cannot acquire style by shoving your writing under the microscope and carefully scrutinizing it. If you peer too closely at your style you will end up parodying yourself. Your writing voice must flow from you naturally, just as your conversational voice does.

Most important, whether your writing style is subtle or obvious, don't feel that you're stuck with it. The writing won't work if there's a clash between form and substance, between *what* you're writing about and *how* you're writing about it. You should be able to change your writing style on a whim, and you must be able to change it to suit the material.

Remember that your primary goal as a writer is not to leave your imprint on the page. Your goal is to *make the writing work*, make it do what it is supposed to do, cause laughter, tears, fright, curiosity . . . .

In the following excerpt from a story I wrote called "The Eight Thou," my goal was to create tension. If I'd tried to write it like Tom Wolfe or Hunter Thompson, I might have looked clever, I might have been funny, but I would not have created tension with all those little side trips. The writing would not have worked. I needed a style of writing that was compatible with tension, that the reader consciously or unconsciously would *associate* with tension.

Test yourself on this.

Think for a moment about tense situations. Delicate brain surgery. The defusing of a bomb. The moment before the jury foreman announces the verdict.

What characteristic do these moments have that you can bring into your writing? (Remember, this is just an example.)

The common denominator that I see in tense moments is a very narrow focus of attention. The eyes and minds of the people involved do not stray; they are locked on a single person or thing, in the present moment. The brain surgeon does not step out for a drink of water. The bomb expert does not break for lunch. The juryman does not catch up on his reading.

When I needed to create tension around my character, Charlie, I employed a writing style that was narrowly focused. I aimed directly at the moment he was in and that narrow spot of territory, his body. No amblings about the date he had last Friday or the house he has in North Miami, no exotic words that would break the tension. I stayed with the here and now.

He began moving again. When he reached the car he shoved the tire iron under the lid of the trunk and put all his weight on it. The trunk creaked loudly. To Charlie it seemed as if the sound screamed like a siren through the dark. He backed off. Nobody came. He crept back out to the car and did it again. Again the sound of creaking metal scared hell out of him and sent him dashing for the safety of the low fence.

For a long time he crouched in the dark, watching the windows across the street. Finally, seeing no signs of curiosity, he went back to the car, shoved his tire iron as deeply as he could get it into the trunk, and with one mighty heave busted the lock. It broke with a shriek of wrenching metal. Charlie dove into the dirt, crawling quickly back to his safe spot in the dark.

For a very long time he waited. His heart pounded furiously. There were no sounds but his own heavy breathing. Somewhere down the block children were laughing, but no one was near. When he was positive nobody was watching from some secret window, Charlie crept back to the car and pushed the trunk lid open. The tire was there.

So was the horribly disfigured body of the late Mrs. Henry Dutros. Charlie was shocked to realize he'd been talking to a murderer all afternoon.

Though I've spoken only briefly about the relationship between style and content in regard to your personal writing style, content will mesh with style in writing that works. We'll see that happen often.

♟ ♟ ♟ ♟ ♟ ♟ ♟   **Coffee Break**

Style as I have used it up to this point and will use it throughout refers to technique—choosing the best word, using the optimum number of words, arranging them in the most efficient and pleasing way. But if you're going to submit your work to editors, you should be aware that to them *style* has an additional, more technical meaning: spelling, grammar, capitalization, punctuation; treatment of recurring elements, and so on. "So let *them* worry about that stuff," you might be thinking. "That's what they're paid for." Nevertheless, a writer whose manuscript shows that he's paid attention to these details will have an edge over a writer who ignores them. And becoming familiar with some of the technical aspects of style will make you feel more like a working writer.

There are dozens of stylebooks you can consult. They won't make thrilling reading; they won't provide creative inspiration. But they will tell you how to punctuate words in parentheses, and whether you should write "the President of the Company" or "the president of the company."

If you skim through several, you'll discover that they don't all agree.

The important thing is not to be "right," but to be consistent. If you get a job writing for a newspaper or magazine you will be told that the publication adheres to a particular style manual, such as the Associated Press Style Book, or the Chicago Manual of Style. This means for that particular publication everything it says in that particular style manual is right and everything else is wrong.

You might think that none of this would seriously touch your life, but when I was a reporter for a regional newspaper here in Massachusetts I was constantly getting upbraided by feminist women who objected to my asking whether they were Miss or Mrs. They pegged me as some sort of anti-feminist sexist pig because my newspaper refused to print ''Ms.''

Part
THREE
The Hidden Work of Words

The Work Words Do

Bill Gagnon, the managing editor of the *UU World*, walked into my office a couple of weeks ago.

"I'm stumped," he said, stroking his beard. "Tell me what you think."

Bill's problem was that the new year was less than a month away, and he wanted to begin his editorial with something about looking back and ahead like Janus, the Roman god of gates and doorways, for whom the month of January was named.

Before he came to me, Bill had agonized over whether the image of Janus at the new year was an unforgivable cliché. (If you don't know why he was worried about using a cliché, jump ahead a few pages, read the chapter called "Avoid Clichés Like the Plague," then come back.)

Certainly it *had* been a cliché. At one time half the high school sophomores on the planet had written Janus into New Year's leads for student newspapers. But Bill wanted me to assure him that, since nobody read mythology anymore, the image of Janus had ceased to be trite and he could use it in good conscience.

No dice.

I said that if nobody knew who Janus was, it would be pointless to use him, but that most readers probably *did* know and so yes, it probably was still a cliché.

But Bill was determined to use Janus, and he wasn't going to let a little thing like my opinion sway him. His editorial began "Here we are in January, standing again with Janus in a momentous present, with one face looking back over the troubled Seventies, the other toward the uncertain Eighties."

Few people would stop to wonder what that word *again* was doing in the sentence. They would assume it just kind of fell out of the typewriter, and if it wasn't helping much, it wasn't hurting anything, either. But that *again* popped off the page at me. It craved analysis. I knew exactly why the word was there, and it was not for any noble reason, such as improving the sentence.

Again was Bill's way of saying "I know, I know. Janus is a cliché. But I am *consciously* choosing to use it *again*, so don't get the idea that I'm some kind of dummy."

If you're just beginning to write, this conclusion might seem incredibly farfetched. But I asked Bill if I was right and he said yes, that's what he was doing. (I couldn't be smug. I spotted it only because I've done that sort of thing myself hundreds of times.)

I tell this story to show you that words can do many jobs besides the obvious one of meaning something. In this case Bill was using the word *again* to convey something more than the word's meaning. He was using the word as a disclaimer, a subtle statement about his understanding of the English language.

If words are employees, as I like to think of them, they are most like handymen. They can disclaim. They can warn. They can remind. They can do hundreds of things, because they have many talents.

A word has meaning, yes, but it also has shape, size, length, sound, characteristics such as rarity or familiarity, and a variety of connotations that have clung to it long before the writer picked it out. Because words, individually and in groups, can perform many chores, you must choose your words carefully, making sure each is pulling its weight and that all are working well as a team. Otherwise they'll do jobs you don't want done. Then they aren't working—they're goofing off.

A continuing theme of this book is the *total writing process*, the relationship between form and content. Form results from words' grouping together. They can be combined in endlessly varied patterns, and each pattern will influence the reader's feelings in a different way. Style, sentence length, sound, punctuation, and other elements you might not have considered—this is the hidden work of words.

In this section we'll consider some of the good work words do, as well as some of the goofing off they do. It's important for you to know, or at least wisely guess, what a word or an arrangement of words will bring to a reader besides meaning.

Once your story or book or article is published, you have no control over how your readers read it. So you must know what a word will "say," not just with its dictionary definition, but with the noise it makes and the ways it's been used in the past.

While this section gives several examples of ways words can work for or against you, it leaves most of the ways unwritten. On your next coffee break, try to think of some jobs words do that I haven't mentioned. Then add your list to mine and consider this: Between us we've come up with only a small percentage of the ways words can tamper with our emotions, expand our knowledge, clarify our perceptions.

When you get right down to it, the matter of *how* words work is a mysterious one. Scientists in a field called psycholinguistics are still trying to figure out just how it is we are able to learn to talk, to read, to recognize words and be able to use them. But mystery or no, you can learn *which* words will work and which ones won't, even if you don't know why or how.

(Here's an example of a special job that I'm assigning a particular word: To keep things simple I'll use the word *story* throughout this section to mean any writing you do—nonfiction articles, novels, books about mushrooms, whatever.)

If the Writer Is Seen at Work, the Writing Won't Work

Consider first the spell cast by reading. You're all alone as you read, yet you hear my voice. You don't know me. I don't know you. But we're both acting as if the other were a real individual composed of flesh and bones. The words that I'm addressing to you aren't being uttered now. They were recorded months ago, perhaps years ago. I might be thousands of miles away. I might be dead. (On the other hand, you might not even have been born yet as I write.)

All you are really looking at is a bunch of black lines that make noises in your head and create a presence that doesn't really exist. It's magic.

Take a moment and think about that spell, that curious suspension of reality that is *reading*. It is particularly true, of course, in fiction. Think of a character you know well from a novel you've recently read. Amaze yourself with the simple yet incredible fact that he doesn't exist, never did. You and the author made him up.

As a writer *you* must try to create and sustain this spell. You must seize the reader's attention and funnel it into your words for the length of the story, article, book, or even press release. You must hypnotize your reader with your action and your information and your style.

Writing works best when you hypnotize the reader quickly and hold him spellbound until you're through with him. You want his attention, and to keep it you must avoid the *distractions* that will cause his attention to wander and the *moments of boredom* that will make him search for more interesting material.

For now let's forget about those boring moments that result from dull writing, and concentrate on the biggest distraction of all:

The writer.

If the writer is seen at work, the writing won't work.

There are words and combinations of words which for various reasons have the effect of reminding the reader that he is reading, that there is a person making an effort to hypnotize him. Just as you sometimes awaken in the morning with the realization "Oh, I was only dreaming," the reader awakens from his spell, saying to himself "Oh, I was only reading." It's the writer's obtrusive presence that does this, just as if he had crept up behind the reader and tapped him on the shoulder.

"See, here I am thumbing through my thesaurus," the writer seems to be saying when he uses a word that is utterly wrong for the sentence.

"Here I am trying to impress you," when his writing gets too wordy.

"Here I am! I'm trying to fool you . . . with all these black lines on paper," when an excess of punctuation or some typographical trick breaks the reader's concentration and reminds him that he's reading.

When the writer is seen at work, the writing doesn't work.

Don't let the reader see you at work. It will shatter the spell. Imagine how you'd react if you saw the director's back as John Wayne was riding off into the sunset. Any one reminder that a writer is at work won't be fatal, but each mistake you make is an interruption of that spell. We all can tolerate just so many interruptions before we abandon an endeavor. The moment you distract the reader, your writing stops working.

This doesn't mean that you can't become a character in your own work, like Hunter Thompson, or leave a distinct stylistic imprint on your writing, as Kurt Vonnegut does. It means you should avoid calling attention to what you're doing, to the effort it entails.

There are occasional exceptions to this rule, times when the writer can be seen at work and the writing will still work. Alliteration and parallel construction, which I'll discuss in detail later, are two examples.

Why do they work?

I have two answers. I'm sure there are more.

I think one reason such devices work is that the writer is being clever. Working under a limited set of rules (such as "Use only words beginning with the letter *P*"), he comes up with an expression that not only suits his purpose, but entertains as well.

We forgive him his interruption and invite him in, just as we'd let a man who does card tricks in for a few minutes even though we're watching television. (But remember, the man who repeats "Pick a card, any card" can get on your nerves in a hurry when you're trying to concentrate on something else.)

Sometimes these devices work because they're hitching a ride in the direction the brain wants to go. The brain accepts some sounds and arrangements of ideas easily and resists others, just as it accepts confused frogs and struggles with "assimilatory coordination between schemata."

These devices work because they don't run against the grain of the brain. There's not room enough here to speculate why the brain accepts some word combinations easily and rejects others. The deep and ultimate answers to the question "Why does writing work?" are imbedded in the cells of your brain and mine. But even if you don't know *why* writing works, you can learn through observation and practice *what* writing works.

The issue of writer intrusion is complex. Sometimes it works because the writer is supposed to be there, because he was a participant in the events he describes, for example, or because he is an expert in the field under dicussion and his opinion would be valuable to the reader. Other times it works because the reader gets something in return for the interruption.

But generally it doesn't work. After all the exceptions are counted and we've made allowances for the grain of the brain and sleight-of-hand in the living room, we can still say, generally, "When the writer is seen at work, the writing doesn't work."

☕ ☕ ☕ ☕ ☕ ☕ ☕ ☕   Coffee Break

This book, by its nature, must break down writing that works into parts for examination and explanation. But the book as a whole should convey to you the totality, the interrelatedness of the writing process. When we talked about the rules of style, I told you that they overlap and that they would show up in different ways throughout the book.

The same goes for "The Hidden Work of Words." Each of these statements about association, intention, punctuation, etc., will contain information about all the others.

Also, relax. To be a good writer you don't have to learn all this in the sense of memorizing everything in the book. There's no quiz at the end. You don't have to scrutinize what you've written with this book in your hand, asking "Did I do this, did I do that?" Just read it, and maybe read it again, and you will begin to observe the workings of your writing and the writing of others.

Now pour yourself a cup of coffee. Find something that you wrote before you started reading this book. Go to your spot that's away from it all and start crossing out words and making changes in the manuscript. You'll find that you're learning more and more about writing, and that the process isn't at all painful—in fact, it's fun!

Avoid Cliches Like the Plague

Cliched. Trite. Hackneyed. These are just a few of the nasty names editors might call some of your favorite phrases. They all mean the same thing: The phrases have been used too many times before; the reader is too familiar with them.

And basically they all suffer from the same problem Robert Redford has if he tries to take his coffee break under the golden arches: they can't sneak in without being recognized. They break the spell, and the reader's concentration.

Just what are they? They're similes (which we'll discuss later) like "clean as a whistle" or "big as an ox," allusions like comparing the arrival of a new year to the god Janus, and plot situations like spoiled boys finding their manhood in love affairs with girls who are dying of leukemia. (These may have worked once or twice, but watch out for the third or fourth.)

Clichés, trite expressions, hackneyed phrases, and worn-out plots don't work.

Why?

They don't work because any time the reader comes upon a word or phrase or plot that he's seen many times while reading, he realizes that he *is* reading. For a fraction of a second the spell is broken.

They don't work because they make the reader think the writer is lazy. Instead of creating something fresh, the writer has gone to the warehouse and picked up Phrase #7 or Plot #22. Instead of an original oil he's giving the reader a painting-by-number.

Obviously, clichés are relative. To the five-year-old who has never read a book, there are no clichés, no threadbare plots. But if you're writing for adults, you're assuming that your readers read, watch television, go to the movies, talk to people, and secretly listen to other people's conversations on the bus. So don't dish out what they've heard a million times.

How do you know which phrases have been overused? The same way your readers do: by reading a lot, watching television, going to the movies, talking, and eavesdropping.

You'll never free your writing completely of hackneyed expressions. You could in good conscience use one that you thought you'd invented, unaware that nine thousand other writers had invented it before you. On the other hand, you might come up with some combination of words that seems so perfectly brilliant to you that you're sure it must have been used by many other writers before you, even though you've never seen it. My advice in that case is, use it.

A Cliché Game

Here are some clichés and overused expressions that writers

often reach for when they lack the energy or imagination to come up with something new. See if you can freshen them up; invent original ways of saying the same thing. For example, you could change the first one to "He's such a good salesman he could make $30,000 a year selling inflatable paperweights."

1. He's such a good salesman he could sell refrigerators to the Eskimos.
2. Sly as a fox.
3. Old as Methuselah.
4. She burned her candle at both ends.
5. Behind the eight ball.
6. Black as night.
7. Out of the frying pan into the fire.
8. He left no stone unturned.
9. Gilding the lily.
10. That hits the nail on the head.

Remember, there's nothing inherently wrong with these expressions. Most of them are good descriptive phrases. It's *because* they were good that they were used over and over and started to get boring, just as a good song can get boring after you've heard it too often.

Associations

My dictionary lists one of the definitions of *associate* as "to connect in the mind or imagination."

One of the ways words work is by causing the reader to connect things in his mind, to associate. Many of the words you use will cause him to make associations. Use words deliberately for this purpose when you can, and edit from your writing all words that elicit associations you don't want made.

These associations cross many lines. A symbol can be associated with something tangible, the figurative with something literal. Something visual, such as punctuation or white space, can be associated with something abstract, such as loneliness.

I spoke earlier about how your writing *style* can be associated with the *content* of your story. Remember Charlie trying to break into the trunk? I used a narrow focus of attention, which is associated with tension, to create the desired mood.

The next example shows how your writing style can be *associated* with the pace of your action.

Think about a disagreement turning into an argument, and then to a fight. As the conflict escalates, things happen at a faster pace. We start off saying "I think you are mistaken on this issue," and finish with "Drop dead."

By quickening the pace of your sentences, shortening them, you can play on the reader's association of faster pace with hotter tempers:

"Coleman swore at Bernstein and told him never to come back into the store. Bernstein shook a fist at him and once again demanded his money back."

They argue for a while. Tempers rise and sentences get shorter:

"Coleman glowered across the room. Bernstein burned with rage."

A little more writing at this pace, and by the time they come to blows, you've pared your sentences down to just a few words:

"Bernstein punched. Coleman kicked. They spat. They clawed. Bernstein screamed. He crashed to the floor."

By translating the pace of the action into the pace of the sentences, you get the reader to "connect [the two] in the mind or imagination."

Now let's consider a distinctly different way of using words to get the reader to associate.

Do you remember in our discussion of wordiness that I said there might be times when using a phrase like "nugatory conjectures" would be a good idea?

Small doses of wordiness are useful when creating a pompous character that you want the reader to associate wordiness with. Consider this:

> Gary thought he was clever, but in truth he was a dreadful writer. His prose was a thicket of overgrown words, and it seemed that he and his twenty-pound dictionary waged constant war against clear and simple language. So he stood torpidly on the pebbled border of the lifeless highway, and once again he found himself making nugatory conjectures.

That would be more than enough for the reader to associate Gary with wordiness, to connect Gary and wordiness in his mind.

Another way to use word associations to reinforce your images on the reader's brain is with figurative terms that the reader will associate with literal terms found elsewhere. In other words, use imagery to remind him of facts.

If you interview a magician he might disappear into the kitchen to get some coffee. If you profile the mayor of Boston it might turn out that he doesn't know beans about budget planning. A famous mountain climber might be high on success. All of these sentences contain figurative words that correspond to literal concepts the reader associates with the subject matter. Use these sparingly. Your goal is not to create puns, good or bad, but to strengthen the flavor of your story.

An "Associations" Game

Try to create figurative descriptions that are associated with literal facts in these situations. I'll give you an example on the first one.

1. A ship's captain getting divorced. (His marriage had run aground.)
2. The death of an alcoholic.
3. A priest junking his car.

4. An outlaw breaking his girlfriend's heart.
5. A dancer attaining success.
6. A writer filling out an employment application.
7. A secretary explaining something quickly.
8. An artist telling a story.

   Take a few minutes with your notebook. Try to think of some more. Then pick up something to read, anything, and try to keep track of the associations your brain makes when it comes upon certain words and phrases.

Tone

   Your writing won't work if the reader doesn't know how he's supposed to feel.

   Memorial services don't work if people giggle.

   Comic monologues don't work if the audience weeps.

   Your writing won't work if the reader doesn't react emotionally the way he "should."

   By *tone* I mean a consistent attitude about the material, an attitude that the writer weaves into his work. He expects the reader to maintain the same attitude for as long as the story lasts.

   In effect, the writer starts off by saying "Please listen to this. It's very serious," or "I don't want to overdramatize this, but it *is* important," or "Hey, let's have a few laughs over this subject."

   The writer sets the tone at the beginning of the piece, and if he does anything to contradict that tone, the writing doesn't work.

   Don't send your reader mixed messages.

   Here are three different leads for an article on photography. Each establishes a different tone, a different attitude.

   The writer announces "Let's take photography seriously."

   If you've ever stood quietly in a darkroom, peaceful in the

amber glow of a safelight, and watched the varied shades of gray stain the surface of photographic paper ro re-create a moment that once was . . . then you know something of the alchemy that lures one to the photographer's craft.

The writer announces "Photography is interesting, but let's not take it too seriously."

From the snapping of the shutter to the drying and mounting of the print, photography is an enchanting mixture of science, art, and magic. And while we might speculate for hours on why Cousin Lloyd would want to become a chiropodist, no such wonderments perplex us when we meet a man or woman who takes pictures for a living. We've all peered through a lens from time to time and with the push of a button brought the inexorable rush of time to a grinding halt. We understand.

The writer announces "Let's smile indulgently at photographers."

Photographers are a queer lot. They stand for hours in the dark, dipping overpriced paper into little tubs of smelly chemicals, all for another glimpse of Amy's first birthday cake. And when the phone rings downstairs they cannot answer it. They've got this thing about letting light into their world.

Once you've set the tone, the trick is to stay with it. Read the third lead and then pretend that the first lead is the second paragraph in the same article.

Can you feel yourself being yanked around? You don't know how you're supposed to feel.

My friend Jan, the one who's a facilitator, is becoming quite a good writer. So I'm sure she won't mind if I use one of her little mistakes as an example of the importance of maintaining a consistent tone.

I gave her a class assignment last year to write about a blind person. In the piece that Jan wrote, the blind man is tapping his way down an alley, when he is surrounded by four thugs. Jan had created an ominous mood or tone, one of terror, the blind man's sense of helplessness. A hand reaches out and pushes the blind man to the ground. Someone kicks his walking stick away. The thugs move in. And as the tension grows, Jan wrote "One of the thugs suggested that they beat him up."

That word "suggested" rang a bell in my head. It didn't work. I knew I was reading. I saw the writer at work.

Why?

Because it clashed with the tone of the piece. *Suggesting* is something done by people who are a little short of power, not by thugs who have a blind man on the ground. When people in power "suggest" things, the word becomes humorous, even ludicrous.

Remember this: The reader is always aware of the words you use and of the fact that you chose to use them. He takes your mistakes seriously. It doesn't occur to him that a word slipped by you or that it jumped onto the page when you weren't looking. If your words are funny, the reader assumes you put them there to make him laugh. If your words are provocative, he assumes you put them there to provoke. He expects your individual words and phrases to be consistent with the overall mood you have created, and if you put in words that make him laugh when you're not trying to be funny, or words that make him sad when you are, you'll create a discrepancy in tone, and the writing won't work.

Such a discrepancy in tone might occur if you assign language to do very different jobs in the same paragraph. It jolts the reader. Consider this:

Oscar Curvels ran like hell. He heard the police behind him. "Stop the bastard!" one shouted. "Shoot him!" Curvels kept running. The pain in his feet grew sharper now, like rods of steel being shoved through the bone. He slammed into the fence before he could stop himself. Then he crawled up, and with aching arms pulled himself over it. He landed with a thud on the other side. As he started running again he heard the first gunshot. He imagined a bullet crashing into the back of his skull. Better a quick death now than ten more years in a cell, he thought. His lungs felt like fire. His heart pounded. His legs were swollen with pain. "Kill him," someone shouted, and he waited again for the explosion in his head. Off to his left a gorgeous amber sunset hung like a lantern in the peaceful azure sky, tossing strands of golden light through clouds of cotton that crouched above the purple peaks of distant mountains. He heard the gunshot. He ran faster. Sweat poured down over his eyes. The wail of a siren grew closer.

That whole sunset business is a discrepancy in tone. It clashes. All along I'm telling the reader to feel tense, feel rushed, feel sore. Then suddenly I change my tone, saying, "Oh, don't worry; there's no rush. Take a minute and relax. Look at that pretty sunset; isn't that something?"

It's a mixed message. The reader doesn't know how he should react. The writing doesn't work.

There's no end to the examples I could give you. But all I can really do is give you the concept of tone, and stress the importance of establishing it clearly and adhering to it faithfully. You'll develop your own ear and eye for this. Just remember that the reader is always reading two things: the individual words and the overall story. Your job is to keep these two in harmony by not contradicting on the word level the tone you set on the story level.

Intention

When I was a teenager and hot to learn such things, I bought a book called *How to Seduce Women*. It was a fifty-cent paperback that I picked up at Nick's Spa.

One morning I had a large breakfast of sausages and eggs, four cups of coffee, and orange juice. Afterwards I went up to my room and read the book. It said that when you bring a young woman home from a date you should sit on the couch with her, snuggle a bit, and then lean down and slip one of her shoes off. The logic of this was simple. Soon she would feel off balance having one shoe on and one shoe off, so she would drop the other shoe. At that point, said the book, she has acquiesced in the act of undressing, and from then on, presumably, seduction would be as easy as winding a clock.

What's wrong?

The sausages and eggs, four cups of coffee, and orange juice.

What about them?

Nothing about them. That's what's wrong.

The fact that I had a big breakfast is irrelevant.

Every time you write something, you announce: There's a reason why I'm telling you this. I told you what I had for breakfast, but I never answered your question: Why is he telling me this?

So don't put in anything without a reason. The reader assumes *intention* on your part when you include a fact. You intend to get back to it, he thinks. You intend to make your character more believable with it. You intend to prove a point.

A lot of beginning writers, when they write true experiences or fiction based on true experiences, have a habit of tossing in all sorts of facts . . . just because they really happened.

That something happened is not a good enough reason to write it into your story. It has to mean something. You can't record everything that took place. You have to choose the actions that move your story along, that nail down your images, strengthen your arguments, propel your characters.

We'll talk more about this when we discuss setting the scene. For now just keep in mind that one of the hidden jobs words do is to tell the reader you had a reason for writing them. So you'd better have a reason.

Music

Each word you write will make *sounds* in the reader's head. So in your writing you should strive for that organization of sounds known as *music*.

Writing works when it plays the tune you want it to, the way you want it played. Just as the sound of each instrument contributes to the quality of an orchestra, the sound of each word you write contributes to the quality of your story.

Of course, the sound of each word varies depending on where it is heard, just as the sound of an electric guitar could be euphonious in a soft rock band but jarring in the midst of the New York Philharmonic.

So read everything you write aloud, and imagine that your ear is a large, taut, and sensitive drum lying on its side. In your mind watch each word fall to the skin of the drum and listen for the sound it makes.

Does it fall softly, like a silk scarf floating onto the surface, where it barely whispers? Does it come quickly out of nowhere, like *pit* or *rap*, seeming to puncture a tiny hole in the drum? Is it a three-foot length of steel chain crashing down, like *manufacturing*, or does it sweep across the drum and gently subside, like *esoteric*? Does it make a ping or a thud? Does it clamp right down on the surface, like *imbed*? Or does it bounce a few times, like *imitate*, before it settles down?

Your overall style of writing makes music, too, and if the tune is not easy to listen to, the writing won't work. You won't have to do much research, however, to find a pattern of word music that's easy to listen to. Just listen to the one that's been working for centuries: human speech.

If you listen to speech carefully, one of the first things you'll notice is that few people have taken seriously their English teachers who said "Every sentence must be a complete sentence with a noun and a predicate," and "Never begin a sentence with *and* or *but.*

Such admonishments are issued by people who don't understand that good writing, writing that works, mimics the patterns of spoken language. And spoken language often goes like this:

"Marry her? I don't know. She's a wonderful person. Cute, too. But marry her? I'm in debt up to my earlobes as it is. And I haven't got a chance of getting a job before July. Still . . . "

Notice, I said good writing *mimics* speech. I didn't say it duplicates it. It hums the music but it doesn't sing the words. The ear and the brain are tuned in to the patterns of language. It is those patterns, the music of spoken language, that you want to duplicate in your writing. To do that keep in mind these generalities about speech:

1. When people talk they vary the length of their sentences. They create a music that the ear enjoys, and you should do the same thing in your writing.

2. When people talk they don't construct all their sentences the same way, with the subject followed by the predicate followed by an object.

They don't say "I painted the front door. I fixed the car. I ate lunch. I went to the movies. I saw *Fantasia.*"

They say "I painted the front door. Then the car was broken so I fixed that. After lunch I went to the movies—*Fantasia* was playing."

So vary the size and structure of your sentences.

(Later, when we discuss parallel construction, you'll see that there are occasional times when a few short sentences can be particularly effective *because* they are constructed the same way. But generally when sentences follow a similar pattern they become boring very quickly.)

3. When people talk they use a combination of complete sentences and partial sentences.

They say: "He asked me to go to the Ice Follies with him. And I don't even know this guy. I mean, he seems nice enough, and I have seen him around a few places. At Dunkin Donuts. And one time I saw him at the laundromat. Nice looking. But why me? He doesn't know me from Jane Fonda, and he wants to take me to the Ice Follies. Must be a really strange guy. Of course, I'll go."

While these examples inevitably reveal information about the words people speak, a subject we'll be discussing later, keep in mind that they are here for the music they make, the patterns. People rarely utter sixty-word sentences, and you shouldn't write them. But speakers do use a variety of short, medium, and long words, sentences, and phrases. You should write the same way.

Sometimes when I can't think of what to write, I think instead of what sounds to make. Passages, especially opening paragraphs, come to me as noises, like dada dada, dadum. Dee, dee da deedeedee, da da. It sounds ridiculous, but it works, and that's what counts. Then I start creating sentences, and when I can't think of a word or phrase I'll plug in some nonsense words just to maintain the rhythmic flow. In time it evolves into something readable. I'd like you to try the process in reverse. Take this opening paragraph from *Freedom at Midnight* by Larry Collins and Dominique Lapierre (Simon & Schuster, 1975), and read about half of it not as words but as sounds. Read it as a bunch of dadees and dumdums, or hum a tune to it.

It was the winter of a great nation's discontent. An air of

melancholia hung like a chill fog over London. Rarely, if ever, had Britain's capital ushered in a New Year in a mood so bleak, so morose. Hardly a home in the city that festive morning could furnish enough hot water to allow a man to shave or a woman to cover the bottom of a wash-basin. Almost without exception, Londoners had greeted the New Year in bedrooms so cold their breath had drifted on the air like puffs of smoke. Precious few of them had greeted it with a hangover. Whiskey, in the places where it had been available the night before for New Year's Eve celebrations, had cost eight pounds—thirty-five dollars—a bottle.

The music of your writing, like its style, is not something you sit down and plan syllable by syllable. It is more like learning to play piano by ear. For the most part you learn to do it without thinking about it. As long as you can truly hear what you've written, you probably won't compose a lot of harsh and grating noise.

There are, however, times when you will deliberately take control of the auditory aspects of your writing and quite consciously arrange the words for sounds you want the reader to hear. You sometimes make these conscious choices when you are writing, picking a word or a phrase for the sounds it makes. More often you will do it in the rewriting, replacing something that "just doesn't sound right." And sometimes you will employ sound-making devices that are so reliable they have names. Two examples are *alliteration* and *parallel construction*.

Alliteration is "the occurrence in a phrase or line of speech or writing of two or more words having the same initial sound; for example: wailing in the winter wind."

Alliteration can be used for silly games like "Say 'seven sickly sailors sailed the seven seas' ten times fast." But in writing it is used to create a pleasant sound here and there, a sound the brain accepts easily.

Don't strain after it, though. If you read a lot and listen carefully to all the words you read, you will learn to use devices such as alliteration effortlessly. At some level of awareness you will observe how it works, and you will put it to work for you. It becomes an unconscious process. I don't sit down and say "Gee, I think I'll use some alliteration in this article." I never even think about it. But a moment ago when I grabbed one of my published articles just to see how often this sound-making device came up, I found in the first paragraph I looked at that someone was "liberated, but lonely," and that something else was "symbolically, if not subtly, summed up." That's alliteration. Use it. But not too often.

Parallel construction, deliberately forming sentences in the same way, is another of those auditory devices that can make a thought more striking to the ear. When the sound is more memorable, the thought itself is more memorable.

Jerome Kern could have written "Fish got to swim, and flying is something that birds have to do." Instead, he, being a composer and needing to make his words work with music, used parallel construction: "Fish got to swim, and birds got to fly. I got to love one man til I die."

If you were a cop drinking coffee down at the station after a drug bust, and you wanted to speak convincingly about how solid the case against the suspect was going to be, would you say:

"We found drugs in the car. The coffee pot contained some drugs. When I opened the medicine cabinet I discovered drugs there, too. In fact, there were several places in the apartment where we found hidden drugs."

Or would you pound your point home by speaking in parallel constuction:

"We found drugs in the car. We found drugs in the coffee pot. We found drugs in the medicine cabinet. We found drugs all over that apartment."

Parallel construction usually means setting up two or more

sentences or phrases in a row so that they will make a similar sound. Why? Because you want to remind the reader that they are alike. Sentences that are built alike land on the ear the same way and they gain a cumulative credibility. Often it's as if you make a statement and then provide the reader with a list of corollaries to prove you're right. Listen to what happens in this passage from my Marilyn French profile. In the first sentence I make a statement. In the next four sentences I use the parallel construction of *they* followed directly by a verb to prove I'm right.

> The stories woven into this novel, which she insists is not autobiographical, are of women enduring from one mundane moment to the next. They have babies. They clean diapers. They pinch their bodies and paint their faces for parties down the street, and they swap souls with other women over coffee in the kitchen. They go to college when their thighs have fattened and spots of gray cling to their fluffy black hair, pressing their lives into an elusive mold called liberation.

Parallel construction makes a nice sound. It works. Use it, but don't go crazy with it.

Incidentally, many times you will find that if you use the same word twice in a sentence, but not in parallel ways, the two will kind of clack together and make an unpleasant sound.

Compare "Individual writers have individual styles" with "Individual writers have styles that are individual."

In the first sentence, the writer used the same word twice to create a rhythm. In the second, the repeated word clashes.

A Listening Game

Do you remember that little meditative exercise we did earlier, when I asked you to pay attention to the subtle ways words affected you? Let's try that again. Go someplace quiet with something you've written.

Relax. Read the words aloud and listen for the tunes they play, the sounds they make, the rhythms. Ask yourself questions: Is this a pleasant tune? Does it have variety? Does it give the reader short sentences so that he can rest, but long and medium sentences so that he doesn't get bored?

Think about that drum. Imagine how the words sound when they land on it. Do they make the sounds you want them to make?

Appearance

The words you write have an appearance as well as a sound. They look like something. They have length, size, shape. They are surrounded by white space and interrupted by little marks called punctuation. The appearance of your writing is one more quality you can use to make it work.

One reason dialogue is so popular is that it is sparse writing afloat in a sea of white space. The typical book browser riffles through the pages of a novel and is attracted by the white space he sees flashing by. Without reading the actual words, he is hooked by the look of the writing.

The white space on a page can also be used to influence the meaning of words. Consider this:

> She had come at last to the end of her marriage. Stan was not coming back, and though she'd known that for months, she knew it now at a deeper level. This feeling that had been growing on her had at last pierced the marrow, and as she stood staring dumbly into an empty bureau drawer that once held his socks and shirts, she gave it a name.
>
> Loneliness.
>
> She was lonely, and for the moment there was nothing; nothing in the world that could end it.

What could be lonelier than one word all by itself on a line?

You can also multiply the importance of a word or thought by putting it all alone on a page.

You won't use such tricks very often, but there are certain visual considerations you will want to take into account more frequently.

For example, don't write things like "Innovative manufacturing engineering techniques accelerate production capacities inestimably." None of these words is particularly obscure, so the usual admonition against wordiness wouldn't necessarily knock any one of them out. The problem is they are all long and cumbersome, and the reader is going to *see* them before he reads them.

It's a little harder to imagine, but if you went overboard in stuffing your book full of one-syllable words, a browser might glance through it, conclude that he's lost in the children's section with a third-grade primer, and shove it back on the shelf.

(Note that while I'm referring to your ultimate readers, the book or magazine purchasers, the reality is that your first reader will be an editor, and he'll be even more critical than they are.)

Punctuation and typography are perhaps the areas where writers most often strive, and fail, to enhance the meaning of their words with visual gimmicks. As a rule, punctuation and typography should be unobtrusive. Like a good butler, they should be there to serve but go largely unnoticed. Usually if you try to do cutesy things with punctuation and type—lots of upper-case letters and so on—you will come across as a moron. I know, I know. Tom Wolfe does it with great success. But he has staked out that particular piece of writing territory and claimed it for his own; to trespass on it would be risky indeed.

Used sparingly, however, unusual punctuation and typography *can* add dimensions to your writing. Long before they had the freedom to portray sex explicitly, clinically, and boringly, writers were able to titillate readers with sex scenes that led to the bedroom door, perhaps even as far as the bed, and then were followed by . . . . . . , which speaks volumes.

Italicized words, such as I have used throughout this book, can make one word in a sentence a little weightier, a little more emphatic, and an exclamation point—judiciously placed, of course!—can certainly enhance the meaning of a sentence.

You'll have to excuse me for a minute while I have a mad screaming fit about exclamation points. They do good work when put to the right task, but so many new writers use them to excess that I am seriously afraid we are going to run out of them.

In my book *The Dorchester Gas Tank*, there appeared a character named Irma Soup. I wanted to portray Irma as something of an imbecile. How did I do it? Simple: I had her write a letter that was bristling with exclamation points. (That's a free lesson in characterization, and we haven't even gotten to the Characterization section yet.)

Nora and I once worked as switchboard operators at the Carillon Hotel in Miami Beach. One of the highlights of our week was the arrival of the activities bulletin, a long list of events at the hotel. We used to make ourselves nearly sick with laughter reading it, because every event was followed by a series of exclamation points that was longer than the event itself:

"Tues. 7:30—Fun With Bingo! ! ! ! ! !" it said, or "Jack Wasserman—Miami's Favorite Comedian! ! ! ! ! ! ! !"

(We also enjoyed the fact that at least six different performers were Miami's favorite comedian.)

Anyhow, the point is that the woman who wrote this thing was having her exclamation points shipped in by the truckload.

She's not going to stop using them, so you should conserve. Use them sparingly, and never use more than one at a time. Don't use exclamation points to call further attention to something you wrote that you think is clever. If it's clever, the reader will notice. If it's not clever, an exclamation point will only make things worse by tipping off the reader that it's *supposed* to be clever. Using exclamation points that way is much like laughing at your own jokes. It is the literary equivalent of television soundtracks that tell you when you're supposed to laugh, or those moronic cavalry charges that tell you when you're supposed to cheer at basketball games.

The most immediate and practical place for you to consider the visual impact of what you write is in the neatness and cleanliness of your manuscripts and query letters to editors. You could write another *Gone with the Wind*, but if it comes in tattered at the edges, stained with instant Sanka, and crisscrossed with black lines that explain what's supposed to go where, it ain't gonna get published. Mainly because it ain't gonna get read.

Your manuscript has to compete with hundreds of others for the attention of an editor who reads all day. The look of it tells him a lot about your attitude toward your writing. It should be attractive to look at. Use a fresh ribbon. Leave plenty of white space in the margins. Double-space. Stay away from gimmicks like purple paper and red ribbons. In short, make anything you send to an editor as visually appealing as possible. However, don't turn into such a lunatic that you retype a page because it has one typing error. A few pencil corrections won't ruin the looks of an otherwise neat manuscript, but many will.

When you get to the publishing stage, a variety of visual elements that you have no control over come into play. There are hundreds of typefaces and sizes, weights of paper, and an infinite number of ways your story or article can be arranged in print. You won't have a voice in these matters unless you happen to be a big-deal writer who's hauling down heavy bucks for the publisher. Then you can call him and say "Listen, Buster, I want it done my way or I walk. Got it?"

♟ ♟ ♟ ♟ ♟ ♟ ♟   Coffee Break

I don't want to tear off on a whole tirade about the shortcomings of society, but if you'll take a quick look at the great social movements of our day—civil rights, feminism, and others—you'll see that the people who lead those movements are well aware of the power of words. Black people have long complained about the negative connotations of the word *black*. We have blackmail and blackballing; things are black as sin; villains are black-hearted; we ruin someone's reputation by painting him black, then we blacklist him, and when he dies we haul him away in a black car. Such associations with *black* cannot help but distress black people.

And feminists have rightly complained that our language reinforces assumptions about the sex of unspecified persons. Our language assumes that everybody is male until he is proved otherwise, unless he is doing a "female" job, such as nursing or teaching.

However, I'm not here to take a stand on feminism so much as I am to tell you that degenderization of language is a major goal of the feminist movement, and it's going to come up in your writing career just as surely as commas and question marks.

There are several stylebooks around that deal with the issue. They recommend such words as *gentlepersons* instead of *gentlemen* (when you're addressing a mixed group or one of unknown gender) and *chair*, or *chairperson*, to replace *chairman*.

For those now-and-then problems you can use such a stylebook, or do what your conscience tells you.

But the common problem, the one that pops up in every paragraph, if not every sentence, is the traditional use of masculine pronouns in reference to a nonspecific antecedent. (A woman has got to watch herself, but a stranger to the city has got to watch himself.) A number of remedies have been suggested to raise consciousness and bring sexual equality to pronouns. *He/she* is one. *S/he* is another. Alternating *him*s and *her*s and *he*s and *she*s is another. For the writer who's a feminist and the feminist who's a writer, they all have one thing in common: they cause conflict.

For the writer they are bad writing: for now, they don't work because they are freaks. They get noticed and call attention to the writing. If I say "The president should call her cabinet together in times of crisis," you get distracted by the fact that the president is female. You assume I made the president a woman for some specific reason.

For the feminist, on the other hand, that's just the point. The feminist *wants* to call attention to the fact that the president might be a woman.

I feel that we should use he and she, him and her more or less equally, though I don't think we should get fanatical about alternating them. The reason the feminine pronouns are a problem now (or masculine pronouns when the antecedent is nurse, secretary, housekeeper, etc.) is that they clash with the reader's expectations. But if we use them often enough, they will become the norm.

So why, you might ask, don't I practice what I preach? Why don't I use feminine and masculine pronouns more or less equally in this book? I did in the manuscript, but my editors, though they agreed it was politically sound, found it stylistically suspect, and decided to use the masculine form consistently throughout.

Which only goes to show you that even a writer doesn't have total control over her work.

Part

FOUR

People

Write Sentences About People

Imagine that three weeks ago you met someone wonderful. The two of you started dating. Then came lingering, affectionate phone calls every night when you couldn't be together. Your special new person sent flowers one day, silly poetry the next. And finally it is that perfect night. The time is right, the place is private, you both feel warm and secure. This person caresses your cheek, looks you in the face, and says, "Love is something I feel a lot of for you."

Yuk!

Wouldn't you feel so much better if she or he had just said, "I love you"?

You don't want a sentence that's about love. Love is a thing, it's an abstract. You want a sentence that's about the two of you. *I* love *you*. That's a sentence about *people*.

You don't need to put a person in charge every single sentence—that would rob your prose of much of its richness and variety. But your writing will work better if you keep returning to a human being, and making him take action. Avoid a long series of sentences in which the person is the recipient of the action. Consider this:

> One minute fury engulfed him because she had come, and angry wishes that her crying would cease, that her departure would arrive soon, filled his head. And thirty seconds later his arms surrounded her, and the knowledge, beyond the shadow of a doubt, struck him that the answer to that nagging feeling of emptiness that had bedeviled him for so long had arrived. It had gone forever and wholeness had come to him again because the one thing lacking had been found by him . . . his own Juli. Not part of his past, but quite suddenly, and for always, a part of his heart.

If you study the sentences in that paragraph, you will see that the writing doesn't work. But it's not because the sentences go against my earlier recommendation to use active voice most of the time. Fury engulfed. Arms surrounded. Knowledge struck. These are active phrases. The reason the writing doesn't work is that nobody is doing anything. Fury is engulfing, arms are surrounding, and knowledge is striking, but no person is taking charge. Which is why M.M. Kaye didn't write the passage that way in *The Far Pavilions* (St. Martin's Press, 1978). She wrote:

> One minute he had been furious with her for coming and wishing angrily that she would stop crying and go away— quickly. And thirty seconds later, holding her, he had known without a shadow of a doubt that he had found the answer to that nagging feeling of emptiness that had bedeviled him for so long. It had gone forever and he had been made whole again, because he had found the thing that was lacking—it was here in his arms. Juli . . . his own Juli. Not part of his past, but quite suddenly, and for always, a part of his heart.

Here is a nonfiction example that is also full of those unpopulated sentences that can make your writing dull.

> The life of a writer is an easy one. The day arrives with late morning naps and leisurely cups of coffee. At noon there are delightful letters to be answered, and around two p.m. there are checks to be snatched from the mailbox. At four o'clock, of course, out comes the silver tea set and in comes a clique of other fascinating and erudite writers. Then, before supper there is the creative thrill that comes with sitting down for an hour or so and rapping out a story or magazine article that will bring in money, praise, and recognition. After supper, when steaks have been eaten and wine consumed, there is that trip to the theater or a party where material is gathered for the next story and the writer is surrounded by the many people who are attracted to his glamorous world.

The problem with that passage, aside from the fact that it's a pack of lies, is that it's not about a person. It's about days and checks and wine and parties.

Even when you are writing about unspecificied persons such as "writers," or "Hudson shopkeepers," or "victims of this heinous crime," you should still write about *people*, give people something to do. Listen to how much more interesting that passage becomes when I create a writer-person to carry out my action.

> The writer has an easy life. He sleeps late in the morning and when he finally crawls out of bed it is to drink leisurely cups of coffee. At noon he answers delightful letters and at two p.m. he runs to snatch the checks out of the mailbox. At four o'clock, of course, he brings out the silver tea set and welcomes his clique of fascinating and erudite writer friends. Just before supper he thrills himself into the heights of creative ecstasy by sitting down for an hour or so and rapping out a story or magazine article that will make him rich and famous. After he dines on steak and wine he goes to a theater or a party where he gathers material for the next story, and basks in the glow of attention from people who find his glamorous world irresistible.

A "Write Sentences About People" Game

The following is based on a passage from *Coma* by Robin Cook (Little, Brown, 1977). I've broken it down into sentences, which I've rewritten so as to take control away from the people. Give control back to people by rewriting the sentences and making people do things. In some cases you will perhaps be doing the same rewriting Cook did when he wrote the book.

1. As the elevator doors began to close, Susan's legs carried her quickly down the corridor, and a mental checklist of the number of doorways she had passed ticked off in her head.

2. Suddenly, in the distance appeared a miniature forklift

loaded with units of whole blood, being driven by a man.

3. An intersecting corridor seemed to be the place from which he appeared.

4. Half skidding and half running was the motion that brought her into one of the recessed doorways, crashing up against a wall, her breath coming in gasps.

5. Her ears awaited sound.

6. The sound of the machine receded.

7. Her eyes searched the corridor.

8. Her strength moved her from the wall and the ninth door was reached.

9. The need to wait held her like a vise until her breath returned to a semblance of normal, before cracking the door and checking the room.

10. Her legs carried her in quickly.

Write Stories About People

It has always seemed to me that the reason many science fiction television shows and movies and stories are so dismally dull is that the writers imagine people will be different in a mere thousand years or so. They load up their scenarios with deadly laser guns and metallic panels that go burp-burp-burp, and they strip their characters of jealousy, lust, glee, love, confusion—in other words, all that is human. Planets where there is no passion and galaxies where no one laughs glut the universes these writers create. Armies of clones and government by machine, cold and loveless, all ignore the basic reason that people go to the movies, watch television, and read.

People.

That's what it's all about. We read to touch other people. To identify with other people. To compare ourselves with other people. To laugh at other people. To see, to hear, to feel other people.

Imagine this: You are in a room with a stack of books, a pinball machine, a cheeseburger, a pile of nice new clothes, and a tub of warm water. And you are lonely. Which comfort source would you turn to? Which can give you that human contact, that people fix you need to take the edge off your loneliness?

What *good* science fiction writers know (and good writers in general know) is that people have been made out of the same stuff for years and they will continue to be made out of that stuff for a long time.

Whether you intend to write science fiction or not, you can learn a lot from reading some of the works of good science fiction writers. You will notice that while technology erupts and erases all the environments familiar to you, recognizable human qualities continue. People are still people, whether they're in Detroit, Afghanistan, or on planet Zip-3.

So good writing is about people. There are exceptions, but fewer than you might think.

The advice to write about people should be taken on at least two levels. There is the word or sentence level, which we have talked about, the stylistic admonishment to put people in charge of sentences most of the time. But writing about people also means writing your stories from a people point of view.

This book is about writing that works in both fiction and nonfiction, so when I say "stories," I mean anything you write that's longer than a sentence. Columns, articles, essays, nonfiction books, short stories, and novels should all be about people.

"Well, novels and short stories, sure," you say. "But magazine and newspaper articles aren't usually about people. They're about the energy crisis or inflation or the new exhibit at the art museum, right?"

Wrong. They are almost always about people. For every article printed about needlepoint there are ten about someone who does needlepoint. For every article about football there are dozens about football players.

Right about now I was going to make a wager. I was going to bet you a nickel that I could grab from the bookshelf three books that appeared not to be about people (books with titles like *Basic Plumbing, How to Draw,* and *Home Canning of Fruits and Vegetables*), turn to any page, and poke my finger at a paragraph that contained at least five words specifically about people. I was going to write the paragraphs, with the people words underlined.

I did grab the books. I did flip the pages. But I'm not going to print the passages. I'd be ashamed. It was too easy. In fact, I spent most of my time looking for a paragraph that *wasn't* loaded with people words.

Anyhow, when I got bored with that I looked through a stack of magazines. Same thing. People, people, people.

Just as an example, consider the computer. Now there's a non-human being if ever there was one. And yet, if you pick up the November 1979 issue of *Esquire* and read William Flanagan's "Home Computers, for Real," an article that is "about" computers, you will find that paragraph after paragraph is enlivened by people. Consider this:

> The computer—and all that it means—is now about to invade the privacy of your own home. Those funny-looking guys with glasses as thick as the bottoms of Coke bottles have managed to make computers so simple to operate that even not-so-brainy kids can use them. And the damned things are now so cheap in price—$500 to about $1,500— that you can't really beg off buying one because they're too expensive.

Flanagan made me read his whole interesting article, not because I'm that hot to know about computers, but because he kept introducing human beings who fascinated me. Here he gave me "guys with glasses thick as Coke bottles," and "not-so-brainy kids." Later he mentioned "the big toy makers," and "Ben Rosen, a financial analyst," even a computer language of the "Dick and Jane" variety.

People bring facts to life. The reader is a person. He wants to see how these facts relate to him as a person.

Writing about people works.

Credibility in Fiction and Nonfiction

This "People" section is about how you create characters that work, whether they are people you make up for your short stories and novels or real people you talk to for articles. I am calling them all characters. The techniques for bringing people to life on paper are much the same for fiction and nonfiction, but there are a few differences that we should get out of the way first.

In writing fiction you must lay down a foundation of believability. In fiction any time a major character acts in ways that seriously affect the plot, the reader must first be primed to believe that "he would do that." This is an important concept throughout writing: Things can't just suddenly appear out of nowhere. Such magic won't work, because the reader will feel cheated.

Psychological background, social forces, and many other elements push your character into one style of behavior or another. You can explain the fictional character's behavior implicitly (in Chapter 2 Ralph is abandoned by his mother, and in Chapter 9 he panics because he's afraid his wife is going to leave him), or explicitly (in Chapter 9 you write, "Ralph was afraid his wife was going to leave him, because that's what his mother had done"). But the point is you must somehow explain in advance why a character would experience such an emotion.

If Ralph gets mugged, you don't have to explain the motivation of the mugger. The reader can make assumptions. But if Ralph spends the next nine years driving across America in an attempt to track down the mugger, you'd better make it clear that something beyond the actual mugging is eating away at him.

Of course, you have to make your characters believable in nonfiction, too. The credibility difference, however, is that in fiction you make characters and their actions believable by laying down that foundation of believability in advance. In nonfiction you don't have to do that. You're telling the reader "This is true," and he has no reason to doubt you, as long as you show him a nice clear picture to prove it.

Consider this segment from an article I wrote about juvenile crime:

David was nine years old when Jerome Miller applied for the youth services post. A pint-sized, freckle-faced kid with a lump of bright orange hair, David lived in Somerville then. Home was a shabby three-room flat which he shared with his mother and two older brothers who slapped him around whenever they felt like it.

David calls his father "gutless." He was a grease monkey who took a one-way ride out of town before David was even weaned, leaving the Mrs. to get by on welfare payments and whatever she could make working behind the counter of a Davis Square bakery.

When I began to work on that article I had planned to follow some kid through the juvenile justice system, from arrest to incarceration or release, and just change his name. The authorities discouraged me, however. They thought a case history would be spotted by somebody. So I invented David. He never existed. He's fiction in a nonfiction article. (I told the reader at the end of the article, after I had achieved my goal.)

I'm not suggesting that you fill your nonfiction with make-believe people, but that you make your characters believable by pointing out that they have real hair color and a certain number of brothers and live in a specific town. You do the same thing in fiction. The difference is that in fiction the reader believes "he would do that" because the character's background points to it, and in nonfiction the reader believes "he did do that" because the writer says he did.

The other major difference between characters in fiction and nonfiction is that in fiction you begin with nothing and you create traits, habits, mannerisms, until you have come up with as much character as you need. In nonfiction you begin with everything (that is, everything you have been able to observe or find out about your character), and from that everything you select the traits, habits, etc., that will help you characterize most effectively.

Characterization in Fiction and Nonfiction

Character is "the combination of qualities or features that distinguishes one person, group, or thing from another," says my dictionary. And *characterization* is "a description or representation of a person's qualities or peculiarities."

Characterization is a word generally associated with the writing of fiction. Short stories and novels, teleplays, movie scripts—all depend heavily on believable, interesting characters to attract an audience. In fiction you *have* to characterize. Your story succeeds only if the people in it fascinate, anger, please, tickle, or otherwise affect the reader.

In nonfiction that's not necessarily true. Your writing can work because you educate, entertain, instruct, or enrage the reader. A story about installing CB radios could work perfectly well without any characterization.

But, as I say, people show up in almost everything you write, so characterization is an important part of writing nonfiction that works. Putting flesh-and-bones people into your articles gives those articles a life and a movement that sets them apart from articles in which no one's heart is beating.

Characters in your nonfiction fall into two categories. Some characters have to be there because your story is about them, as in interviews with Nobel Prize winners and profiles of famous jugglers. Other characters don't have to be there, but you add them to give your article greater dimension and color; for example, you might spend three hours with a hypnotist and describe her workday for your article on hypnotism.

The newspaper and magazine profiles you remember are the ones in which the writer used characterization, "a description or representation of a person's qualities or peculiarities." Often it is characterization that makes the difference between a dull piece and one that sticks a lasting image on the reader's brain.

My slant on a local politician was that he was loved or hated; few people were neutral about him. One of the paragraphs I used to build this image was:

> Sitting on a board where some torture the English language without mercy every Monday night, Dyer speaks clearly, coolly, and as precisely as a professor. A singer and actor in high school, Dyer polishes off each syllable before he delivers it, and if his rhetoric is often critical, haughty, and downright nasty, it is at least interesting. Things are rarely good or bad when Dyer describes them. Charges made against him have been "dilatory," some committee recommendations have been "abhorrent," and local merchants have often been "munificent" in their service to the town.

Obviously, in an article about Mr. Dyer I had to characterize him at least to some extent. But in 1975 when I was assigned to write about small dairy farming, I didn't have to characterize; I didn't have to populate the piece with visible human beings. I could have stuck to the price of milk and feed, state dairy regulations, and the modernization of farm equipment. But I thought a reader who was stretched out on an easy chair in a downtown high-rise could relate to dairy farming better, and care more about it, if I wrote:

> Paul Schultz of Bolton is a good-looking young man. He talks quietly, and when he moves it is with the ease of a conditioned athlete. But he's not an athlete—he's a dairy farmer.
>
> At 27, when the kids he grew up with are out making eight bucks an hour, feelings that defy explanation keep Paul bound to a lifestyle for which almost nothing good can be said. He works harder than a stevedore, earns less than a secretary, and he can't even get insured against the livestock diseases that could wipe him out tomorrow.

Don't Take More Than You Need

A lot of writers have a hard time catching on to the idea that writing that works is not the creation of real life on paper. It's not surprising, when you consider that people like me are constantly badgering them to "write about real people," "listen to the way people really speak," and "watch for the way things really happen, the way people really gesture, walk, laugh."

But that doesn't mean you have to capture all of life as it occurs during a single moment at a single place and imprint the image on a piece of paper the way you would with a camera.

It means you should find the words that will connect with the contents of the reader's mind to create an illusion of real life.

The writer chooses the words that will unlock memories the reader didn't know were there.

The writer steers the reader's brain onto a few of the millions of tracks available to it.

And, if I might switch metaphors just one more time, the

writer merely begins the drawing; the reader extends the lines.

This message applies to writing in general, and we will discuss it in detail in "Description That Works." For now it means that you create visible, believable characters not by telling the reader *everything* about the character, but by drawing in the part that will make him extend the lines in the direction you intend.

Because the reader is doing most of the work of creating character, you don't have to use many words to characterize minor players in your stories.

In his *Esquire* article on home computers William Flanagan referred to "those funny-looking guys with glasses as thick as Coke bottles" who he said have managed to make computers simple, and the reader could immediately envision an entire army of computer professionals researching and inventing all over the country, an army composed of every computer type the reader had ever encountered in life and in reading.

In that article I wrote on juvenile crime I interviewed a cop by the name of Norman Dubrule. He was just a small part of the article, so I had no intention of telling the reader how Dubrule walked or talked, or what he had for breakfast. But I did want to characterize the police in general in regard to my subject, so after I quoted Dubrule saying "but whether kids go to jail is not our decision. We're supposed to bring them there so that's what we do," I wrote:

> Dubrule's got 23 years in juvenile behind him. He's seen a crushed skull or two, so he's a bit skeptical about the value of any juvenile justice system that doesn't require jail cells.

With that I hoped the reader would extend the lines, would draw on all his images of cops who think the court system is too lenient, and create a nice clear picture.

In the case of Vic Dyer, the local politician, I had to characterize more fully because Dyer was the subject of the article. But even then I characterized in small pieces. In the example I gave you, I concentrated only on his speech patterns. Yet chances are you extended the lines, and saw a lot more of him than I really showed, because you scanned your mental file for all the images you have of people who talk that way. Perhaps you came up with a tone of voice, hand gestures, manner of dress. And you will cling to that picture until I reveal new little bits of characterization to alter your image slightly. And if I carefully choose what it is I want to show you about Vic Dyer you will extend the lines the way I want you to, and the writing will work.

So to make characterization work you don't need to pile detail upon detail. You need to carefully choose some telling characteristics and present them in a lively, interesting manner.

Typecasting

For several months now I have been having an affair with a woman whose husband is a linebacker for the Green Bay Packers.

What do you think? Do you think my wife knows about the affair? Do you think the woman's husband is a big, mean guy who will squash my head like a grape if he finds out? Do you think there is something wrong with my marriage and the woman's marriage? Do you think the whole thing is conducted in secret while he's off cracking heads with the Los Angeles Rams?

How would your answers change if I told you I was having an affair with a woman whose husband is a bookkeeper for a small-town bank? Or if I told you I was having a friendship with the woman?

It's possible that my wife thinks the affair is a great hobby for me. It's possible that my lover's football-playing husband is the unjealous sort who thinks I'm great fun to have around.

It's possible, but not likely.

Most likely when you read the original sentence you assumed

the affair was secret, and you assumed that the football player would resort to violence if he found out. You made those assumptions not because you necessarily believed they would be true in every case, but because you knew those were the prevailing images: affairs are secret, football players are violent; and you also knew that I was trying to tell you something. So your response is based on the attitudes of society, which you assume you share with me, and you will hold onto them until I start adding facts that tell you this instance is different.

It doesn't matter if I think affairs among the married are not improper or if this particular football player is a meek sort who wouldn't step on a cockroach. If I'm proposing something that contradicts the accepted social image, I have to tell you. If I'm not, then I don't.

The reader will assume that your billionaire oil baron is a conservative who votes Republican until you explicitly state that the guy is actually pouring all his money into the Socialist party.

The reader will assume that your unescorted woman, wearing a tight red dress and high heels, sitting in a sleazy bar, is a cheap pickup or a prostitute, until you explicitly state that the woman is a happily married local librarian who just stepped out for a drink.

The reader will assume that your group of black youths hanging out at night on a downtown street corner are up to no good until you explicitly state that they are a basketball team waiting for a bus to take them to a charity game.

Whether you agree or disagree with the reader's sexist stereotypes, racial prejudices, class assumptions, etc., you still have to take them into account.

The images in the reader's mind are the only images you have to work with. If he thinks that your unescorted woman in the bar is a cheap pickup, then that's what you're going to convey when you present such a situation, whether you like it or not. What's worse, even if the reader doesn't feel that way, he thinks that *you* think he does, so when he asks himself the question "What is the writer trying to tell me?'' he comes up with the same answer until you tell him more.

You can't call up the reader and say, "Gee, you shouldn't feel that way." The point is he *does* feel that way, and you have to write accordingly. If you don't want your reader to see the woman in the bar as a cheap pickup, then you must use more words to explain that such is not the case, or avoid characterizing her that way in the first place. Don't call her "unescorted." Don't say the bar is "sleazy." Don't describe the dress as "tight." Ignore the high heels.

Instead, mention the librarian's horn-rimmed glasses, her wedding ring, the delicate way she sips her drink, and her constant use of five-syllable words.

The choice is yours.

There is no such thing as objective characterization.

My definition of *objective* here is the third in my dictionary: "uninfluenced by emotion, surmise, or personal prejudice."

The reason is simple. Every time you write something, a word, a phrase, a sentence, you *could* have written something else . . . and the reader knows it. You said the woman was unescorted when you could have said she was overweight. You said the youths were black when you could have said they were seventeen years old. You said the woman was married to a football player when you could have said she was blind in one eye. The reader assumes, quite logically, that you chose to tell this fact instead of another for a reason. He assumes you had an *intention*, which we discussed in "The Hidden Work of Words."

Until you tell the reader otherwise, he assumes you want him to typecast. That is, he thinks you've chosen to tell him characteristics that are "typical of people like this" so that he can go searching through his mental "types of people" file that has been established by real life, other books, neighbors' comments, television and movies.

Since the reader assumes you write with his stereotypes in mind, since he is going to act *as if* you do, you have no choice but to comply, or your writing simply won't work. The reader is running the show. The communication takes place in his head.

Your writing would become pretty dull if you tried to make all your characters conform to the types the reader carries around in his brain (that is, if you made all your ministers compassionate, your interior decorators prissy, and your female truck drivers mannish). The reader's first image is usually the stereotype; you can use that as a springboard to your own twists of characterization. If you write "Edna took in stray kittens, and she often baked cookies for the neighborhood children," you show the reader that Edna is a type: nice, sweet, gentle. If you write "Edna loved children and kittens, but she liked to go out late at night and slash the tires of cars that burn too much gasoline," you're still using that nice, sweet, gentle type as the standard from which Edna deviates. In other words, you use the type as a way of showing how your character is different.

So give your characters traits that you think readers find typical of the kind of person you want them to see. If your character is like the type, then you've characterized well. If the character is not like the type, then write about the traits that make him different.

Can Bad Guys Be Courteous?

In his excellent book on writing, *The Craft of Fiction*, William C. Knott uses a character named Jenkins to make a few points about characterization. Jenkins is a heavy, overbearing oaf of a man, a grabber, a pusher. Knott puts him through a few scenes to show how these qualities of Jenkins manifest themselves in little actions like buying a movie theater ticket, stopping at the candy counter, etc. Then Knott writes:

Sink into Jenkins' consciousness for a moment. Walk with him down the dim aisle of that theater. He is already munching on that chocolate bar as he starts into a row, his eye on a vacant seat in the center. He is anxious to sit down and watch the picture and as a result doesn't give the old lady sitting in the first seat a chance to get her tiny feet out of the way. He steps on one, crushing it beneath his heavy boot. The old woman cries out.

Now. What does Jenkins do? Does he apologize?

Of course not. You and I both know better than that. If he utters anything even close to an apology it would be completely out of character.

That's what William C. Knott wrote, but on my copy of the book from the Marlboro Public Library some naughty person had penciled in, "Why? Even bad guys can be courteous."

Yes, of course bad guys can be courteous, and there might be times in Jenkins's life when he does apologize to a woman for stepping on her foot. But this toe-stepping episode is presumably not crucial to the story. It is only there in the first place to demonstrate certain insensitive characteristics of Jenkins. Knott put it there to show us an aspect of Jenkins's character, and if Jenkins were going to apologize to the woman, the incident would not have been mentioned. Knott didn't tell us what Jenkins had to eat for breakfast or what color socks he wore, either. He just selected some of the incidents and traits that would cause us to imagine the character he wanted us to imagine.

Bringing Your Characters to Life

We've talked so far about what characteristics to use. I've said you shouldn't pick your characteristics or characteristic incidents at random but rather select specific details that will illuminate the particular aspects of character you want to get across. But you can't characterize well simply by choosing well. You've also got to write well; you've got to present your characters in vivid, interesting ways so that the reader will care about them. That brings us back to those rules of style I said would pop up again. Here are some of them and how they apply to characterization:

Be specific. Which character can you see better, the general man who is "tall," or the specific man who "stands six feet, four inches"?

Which character can you see better, the general man who "doesn't do well, even at small things," or the specific man who "can't even lick the flap of an envelope without cutting his tongue"?

Use active voice. Don't write "Success comes easily to her." Write "She succeeds at everything she does."

Don't write "His eyes become wet with tears whenever he is reminded of Linda." Write "He remembers Linda and he weeps."

Show, don't tell. Whenever possible, have the character come out and demonstrate his trait rather than telling the reader about the trait. When characterization is kept very short this is not always possible, because showing character usually takes a few more words than telling about character. But showing works much better, so do it when you can.

Instead of telling the reader that the boss is a grouch, show him: "The boss snapped at his secretary"; "The boss roared at his salesmen."

Instead of telling the reader the congresswoman was dishonest, show him: "Representative Lewis perjured herself before three committees; she received over $70,000 in bribes, cheated on her income tax for seven years straight, and arranged to get 3,000 votes from people who were dead."

Notice again, it is the verbs that bring your characters to life.

A Game to Show Character

Make a list of one-word characters, such as golfer, acrobat, divorcee, singer, mayor, and mother.

Now, without thinking about those characters, make a list of personal adjectives in front of that list, such as irate, depressed, lame, sentimental, and insane.

You now have a list that looks something like irate golfer, depressed acrobat, lame singer, sentimental mayor, and insane mother.

Try to write a sentence or two that *shows* what each character is without telling the reader. Don't use any of the words on your list. Try to show an irate golfer without using the words *irate* and *golfer*.

You could write something like "He stormed across the fifteenth green swinging a five iron at the reporters."

Any time you can show your characters instead of telling about them, your writing will work better.

Just remember that *what we do springs from what we are*. Every action we take results from some trait we have. The trait need not be a profound or intense one. A man might *run* because he is *tardy*. A mother might *yell* becasue she is *irritable*. A congresswoman might *perjure*, *receive* (bribes), and *cheat* because she is *dishonest*. But every deliberate action results from or manifests something about the character taking the action. Simply ask yourself what he would *do* because he *is* this way, and you will find ways to show your character's traits.

Description as Indirect Characterization

Everything you write delivers a message to the reader, whether you intend it to or not. This doesn't mean that every word is a problem. It means that you should ask yourself if a word or phrase you write is going to deliver a message you don't want delivered. Sometimes when you say things "just because they are true," you accidentally deliver messages that contradict what you really want to say. If you interview a successful Baptist evangelist one morning and there just happens to be an empty whiskey bottle on his desk because the janitor left it there, you can't write it into your description and expect the reader to accept it at face value as just part of the scenery.

If you write "A maroon curtain hangs behind the Reverend Wilson, and the surface of his desk is cluttered with papers and prayer books, an empty whiskey bottle, copies of his new record album, and a Bible signed by the President," the reader will assume that you're trying to send a message with that whiskey bottle. The reader doesn't think you mentioned it "just because it happened to be there." The reader thinks you mean it to say the Reverend Wilson is a drunk, or a hyprocite, or something.

Physical characteristics can deliver messages as quickly as empty whiskey bottles, so be careful in deciding which ones to include.

In the Typecasting chapter I said that if you mention a woman's tight red dress and her high heels, the reader will picture her one way, but if you mention instead her horn-rimmed glasses, he will picture her a different way. The reader asks himself "What kind of a person would *choose* to wear this?" (do this, say this, etc.), and his answer derives, logically, from the prevailing societal attitude.

At first you might think that when you include a descriptive detail that doesn't result from a *choice* the character made, then no characterization takes place. For example, if you tell your reader a girl got hit by a car, he can't find a character type file in his brain for "girls who get hit by cars," because anybody can get hit by a car, regardless of personality. He doesn't make assumptions about this girl until you tell him more.

Logically, then, if you write that a woman has a scar on her face because she got hit by a car when she was twelve, your reader wouldn't draw any conclusions about her character because he knows that anybody can get a scar on his face, regardless of personality.

But our physical appearance, whether we choose it or not, has such an influence on our personality and our motivations that you cannot help but characterize when you describe. The reader has a thin file marked "girls with scars on their faces," and it says that such girls felt ugly in high school so they didn't get asked for dates, and they're still shy with men. It says that they were ridiculed by the other kids, and it made them insecure. So if your character with the scar is sought-after and secure, don't mention the scar "just because it is there," unless you're prepared to provide information that will dispel the reader's "girl with a scar on her face" type.

This is a serious problem in both fiction and nonfiction. In nonfiction the reader has to find an answer to the question "Why did the writer mention the scar?"; in fiction the question is "Why did the writer *put* the scar on the girl's face?" In either case, the reader assumes there is a reason. Many a fiction writer makes the mistake of adding the scar just because he's basing the character on somebody he used to know who just happened to have a scar.

This whole process applies in varying degrees to all physical description. If you say a woman is fat, the reader assumes she is gluttonous and perhaps jolly. If you say a kid has pimples all over his face, the reader assumes he is shy. If you say a man is tall and broad-shouldered, the reader assumes he is aggressive and confident.

If you must employ physical description that will lead to faulty assumptions, try to erase the false image as quickly as possible:

"Though her face resembles a recently sighted asteroid, she has more men chasing her than Farrah Fawcett."

"Though he's big and broad-shouldered, he shrieks with fright at the sight of a mouse."

"Despite his uncanny resemblance to Burt Reynolds, he has never been at ease with women."

The Universal and the Specific

A girl I once dated told me that when her mother nagged her to eat everything on her plate by saying "Millions of people are starving to death in China," she would reply "Name one."

If her mother had been able to name one, the plate might have gotten cleaned.

That's because the girl would have felt guilt, sympathy, pain—whatever her mother was trying to get across.

The reason is that each of us is one single person. Each reader is an individual who identifies with other individuals, not with masses.

When you watch the eleven o'clock news, which bad news troubles your sleep more, "Forty-two people were killed in Iowa when a westbound train derailed near Davenport," or "One of the passengers, seven-year-old Jeffrey Wells, of Waterbury, Connecticut, was found dead with his teddy bear clutched in his arms"?

Who do you *feel* something for?

It's hard to feel for the forty-two nameless, faceless people, but it is so easy to cry for the seven-year-old Jeffrey.

Usually when you write you'll be trying to make your readers feel positive things for your characters: sympathy, concern, friendship. Sometimes you'll want your readers to experience negative emotions: hate, disrespect, revulsion. In either case, you want the readers to *feel* something about the character, just as you felt something about Jeffrey that you did not feel about the forty-two passengers.

To make your readers feel something for your character, you must make your character a specific person. You must find that teddy bear so that your character emerges from forty-two passengers as an individual. You must show some *specific* characteristics.

But the *feeling* you're trying to elicit in your readers is just the opposite. You've never met your readers, so you must strike a chord you know to be *universal*.

Find the specifics of character that unlock a universal emotion.

I'm a man. How is it that as I read about a woman who is frightened as she approaches childbirth I can feel for her and care about her? I can't reach back into my experience memory and find childbirth. I can't even find a trip to the hospital. But I can reach back into my *emotional* memory and find *fear*; we have all experienced fear, if not over childbirth, then over something else. Fear is universal.

Your readers may never have lost a dog, as the boy in your story has, but they have probably lost something. They have known the universal sense of *loss*.

If you interview a congressman who is running for the Senate, find the characteristics he has that demonstrate his ambition. All of your readers won't run for the Senate, but all of them have experienced *ambition*.

If the bank president uses a lot of six-syllable words because he's insecure, then put them in the story. Your readers may not know many six-syllable words, but they understand *insecurity*.

Much of writing has a mirror-image effect. The writer has an image in his mind, which he translates into words. The reader sees the words and translates them back into an image. The writer of fiction asks "If I felt nervous" (universal feeling) "what might I do?" (specific action). So he creates a character who wrings his hands while he talks. The reader comes along and sees a character wringing his hands and wonders "Why is he doing that?'', which is another way of asking ''How would I be feeling if I were doing that?'', and concludes, ''Oh, he's nervous.''

Your story won't be destroyed if a character who isn't nervous wrings his hands. ''Make every word count'' doesn't mean load every word with Significance. But every word you write *is* an opportunity to improve the whole, and writing works best when the largest number of wise, thoughtful choices are made.

Keep in mind, too, that writing is always an act of faith. You write something in the belief that the reader will understand what you're talking about. In the case of characters and their feelings, you're safe. If you once felt something basic, primal, something that wriggled in your soul, you can be sure the reader has felt it, too, and all you have to do is find the characterization that will show it to him.

What to Look For

Everybody you meet is a potential character. If you write nonfiction, you will interview hundreds of people for articles and books. If you write fiction, you will conduct fewer formal interviews, but you should regard *all* conversations as interviews because many of the people you meet—at parties and churches, hospitals and supermarkets—will become characters in your stories. You will want to remember what they said and how they said it. You should approach each encounter with a keen eye and a cocked ear. Keep a checklist in your mind. Everyone has a particular way of talking, dressing, moving, so watch and listen carefully.

Pick out only the useful characteristics, the ones that will work. But first, you must observe *everything*, so that you'll have something to choose from.

Here's a checklist to keep in mind when listening.

Vocabulary. Does she use a lot of long words? Does she use a lot of professional jargon? Does she use certain words often?

Style of speech. Does he speak with authority, or does he sound as if he's not sure? Is he controlling the conversation or are you? Is he trying to manipulate you into asking the right questions? Does he water down all his statements with mitigating phrases like "generally" or "much of the time"?

Tone. What does her voice sound like? Is it melodious? Is it harsh? Is it the same voice she used to talk to the secretary when she was interrupted, or is she putting on a voice for you?

Diction. Does he speak clearly, or mumble into his beard? Does she have an accent?

Once in a while, if I anticipate a particularly long interview, I will bring a tape recorder. But I also bring a notebook. The tape can only record sound. My notebook records everything else on my mental checklist. Here is the kind of checklist you should have in your head whenever you interview someone, or even meet someone who might become a character in your fiction.

Clothing. Do the person's clothes tell how rich or poor he is? Does her manner of dress show that she is careless or careful about detail? Does she dress in good taste? Does he look comfortable in the clothes he is wearing, or is he really a poor boy dressed up like he's a rich boy?

Jewelry. Does she wear a watch, or is time not important? Is the jewelry expensive, ostentatious, sentimental? Is it religious? Does it indicate some other belief, like a pendant that's an astrological sign, or perhaps membership in some organization? Is he forty-two years old and still wearing his high school class ring?

Grooming. Does she wear too much makeup? Or does she glow with good health without makeup? Are her nails long and alluring or short and functional? Are they bitten down? Does he dye his hair? Does he care about his figure?

General appearance. What about posture? Does she slump in the chair or sit up straight? Does he smile a lot when he speaks? Does he gesture with his hands? Is she saying "come closer" or "go away" with her stance? Does he have a big nose, or an intractable pimple that might affect his feelings about himself? Does she reach out and touch you when she speaks?

These are all attributes that would not show up on your tape recording. You can observe them without asking a single question. When sprinkled throughout an article they give it a life that spoken words, no matter how revealing, cannot provide.

Beyond these more or less objective observations you make while your subject is talking, there is, of course, the whole range of *what* he said, and what it discloses. I haven't talked much about that, because it will be covered in "The Words People Speak." The words people speak reveal more about their character than anything else.

The one major area from which character emerges is, of course, the subject's history. Was he abandoned as a child, and how does that affect him now? Was she the queen of the prom and the star of the girls' basketball team? What character traits have resulted from these experiences? The answer to the question "Where do I look to find clues to character?" is "Everywhere."

Part

FIVE

The Words People Speak

Other Voices in Nonfiction and Fiction

If you search long enough you will find short stories and articles in which there is no "voice" but the author's, no words between quotation marks. But you won't find many. Writing that works owes much of its success to those words—either real or imagined—spoken by other people, other characters.

In nonfiction those words come in the form of *quotes*, the actual words of a person who had something to say about the subject at hand. Sometimes the quotes take the form of a conversation between two or more people, but usually they're the words of an individual replying to a question asked by the writer.

In fiction the words of other people are called *dialogue*, conversations usually between two people, though characters do sometimes talk to themselves or to people who aren't there or who don't reply.

Certainly there are other differences between the spoken word as presented in nonfiction and fiction. But of greater importance to the writer are the *similarities* between nonfictional quotes and fictional dialogue.

Quotes and dialogue both break up the page visually and attract readers.

Quotes and dialogue both create space for opinions other than the author's.

Neither quotes nor dialogue automatically becomes interesting just because it sounds as if somebody is really talking. The writer's goal *is* to create the illusion of spoken language pouring forth naturally from the speaker. But that language must be so packed with drama or information or wisdom that a real listener would lean forward to catch every word.

Of course, not every quote can be the epitome of pith, nor can every exchange of dialogue cut directly to the core of an issue.

But the writer can strive always to use the words of other people in the best way at the best times.

Why Quote?

Red is a very exciting color.

A friend of mine says red is a very exciting color.

"Red is a very exciting color," says Jim Bellarosa.

Which of those three sentences did you find the most interesting? Probably the third. The first sentence is about red, and it's interesting only if you happen to be fascinated by the color red. The second sentence concerns a conversation about the color red, and you probably got a little more interested because conversations are more interesting than colors. But the third sentence is about a person who finds the color red to be exciting, and even if you don't care about red, you do care about people.

By using quotes in your nonfiction you often lift the reader's attention level by switching from "the topic" to a "person's words and feelings about the topic."

I'm going to assume that you don't have any particular interest in table hockey. As you read this excerpt from an article I wrote about table hockey, pay attention to your interest level, the degree to which you care about what you're reading, and feel what happens to your interest level when you're reading the quotes.

Steve Bernstein's a good-looking young man. Tall, dark-haired, and broad-shouldered, he could pass himself off as a big-league baseball pitcher.

"I think I'll play this game all my life," he says, "and when I die maybe I'll have my table hockey set buried with me."

Table hockey lore flows from him like a well-paced sermon. His hands take slap shots at the air while his wrists snap in the quick rotating motion needed to get his left wing or defenseman into position.

A smile flashes on his face when he talks table hockey. Maybe it's because he's good at it. Very good.

This is a game that makes beginners look as if they've suddenly contracted some muscular disease which attacks the wrists, forearms, and fingers. The puck zigzags all over the "ice" like a crazed mouse. You've got to get one of two hands to one of six rods during that fleeting second that the puck is near enough to a player for you to shoot, pass, or block a shot.

But Bernstein, after 17 years of playing table hockey, puts his little metal men through their paces like a Parris Island drillmaster.

"You know," he says, "I'm so into this game that I talk to myself about table hockey when I'm driving my bread truck. I go over the games I play and bawl myself out for the stupid things I've done. You know, like lagging on defense or rushing my shots, not taking enough time to set up."

Because he makes a few more mistakes than a couple of guys in the Midwest who eat, breathe, and sleep table hockey, Steve Bernstein is not the best player in the country. But he's never finished lower than fourth in a major table hockey tournament, and if there's a better player on the East Coast, his skills are a well-kept secret.

"One of the things I do wrong is I burn myself out," Bernstein says. "Some of these tournaments run for 12 or 16 straight hours and I roll up a big score early, but I don't have anything left when it gets down to the final rounds. I tire, and I end up finishing third or fourth. I've got to learn to pace myself better."

Did you find you became more interested in table hockey because Steve Bernstein obviously cared so much about it? If you did, then the writing worked.

Using quotes in nonfiction makes a topic human. It brings the topic into the reader's world by introducing him to a real live person who has something to say on the subject.

Another reason to use quotes in nonfiction is to make the story easier on the eyes. Quotes are usually contained in short paragraphs. They break up the big blocks of print and make the page more attractive.

Quotes also give an opinion credibility. I could do research on earthquakes and write "New Jersey is going to split in half and sink into the Atlantic Ocean by this time next year," but that's only a freelance writer expressing his opinion based on a few weeks of research. Wouldn't your interest rise if I wrote " 'New Jersey is going to split in half and sink into the Atlantic Ocean by this time next year,' says' Harold Peck, the world's leading earthquake expert." Credibility.

Another major reason for using quotes in nonfiction is one I've already talked about: characterization. If the story is about the person himself, rather than his business, hobby, situation, etc., then what he says and how he says it is your most valuable asset in showing the reader what he is like.

I've said before that writing that works is writing that does many jobs at once, and I think if you'll reread the Steve Bernstein quotes you'll find that they do all four of the jobs I've mentioned. They humanize the topic, they visually break up the page, they give the subject credibility, and they characterize.

Selecting the Quotes

Ninety percent of the research you do comes in the form of quotes. Either somebody said it to you, or you read it. The only research that doesn't arrive in the form of quotes is your personal experience.

Logically, then, your entire article could be written in quotes. You could excerpt a book you read, follow the excerpt with the words from an expert, toss in a man-in-the-street view, a few appropriate lines from a poem, and maybe some statistics from the bureau of something or other. *You* wouldn't actually say anything. Chances are you'd end up with an article six times as dull as a Tuesday afternoon in Elgin, Illinois.

That's because you would have overlooked the most important expert in any story. The communications expert. You. The people you talk to say good stuff, but they don't say stuff good. They have interesting things to say, but they don't always say them in an interesting way. They might know about home computers, but they don't know about active verbs, showing instead of telling, being specific, varying sentence length, characterizing, and all the other techniques of writing that works. That's your area of expertise. You are the writer.

There is no scientific method of choosing which words to quote and which to use as background information. You use quotes in a story for all of the reasons that you use any other words: variety, sound, association, and so forth. There is no "right" time to throw in a quote. You have to train your ear and your eye to get a sense of how many quotes an article can accommodate, and that depends pretty much on how interesting your speaker is.

But when you do quote, to create that rhythm, that balance, use quotes that serve a specific purpose and can accomplish it better than you could with your own words.

To provoke. Your writing will work any time you can make the reader eager to argue with the person you quote, or get the reader to say to himself "I'm glad he said that; I've been feeling that way for years."

Says Duke: "White people today are facing more massive racial discrimination than the blacks ever faced. We are the only group standing up for whites in this country." (*Time*, November 11, 1979.)

Humor. Many of the people you interview will say one or two witty things during the course of your conversation. Try to use them.

"Some people say the only way to get a Unitarian Universalist to bow his head is to tell him his fly is open," says the Reverend Mack Mitchell, "but that's not true. UUs do pray, but they always begin, 'To whom it may concern.' " (An article of mine in progress.)

Color. Quotes often provide a flavor that is peculiar to a region or a profession.

"Glenn just up and killed himself for nothing is what he did," says the local barber, Kay Young. "People here'd like to see it dry up, not have any more do about it, see what I mean?" (Marguerite del Guidice, the *Boston Globe*, March 9, 1980.)

To stir an emotion in the reader. You want your reader to feel something for your people. Sometimes the best way is a quote.

"I've got to have help," I said, and three or four of them started digging. I was panicky by then, saying, "Oh please God, he's got to be there." And when I looked down this guy crawls out from the hole and he says, "There's nothing there," and I said "He's got to be" and he said no and tears rolled down his face. (Mel Allen, "The Day Kurt Newton Disappeared," *Yankee*, September 1979.)

To characterize. Quotes that characterize do double duty. The words provide information, and the choice of words and the ways in which they are used often tell the reader much about the speaker.

"Everybody's treatin' me like a product, wantin' to write books about me, wantin' to write my life story," she said anxiously. "It's my life. It should be my book, my story. But I ain't lived yet. I'm just beginning to live. What right have you got to tell my story?" (Alanna Nash, "Goodbye Dolly," *Writer's Digest*, July 1979.)

So select quotes that work hard for you, that do some job beyond providing the surface information. If the person you interview is a butcher, a baker, or a candlestick maker, it is highly unlikely that he is going to be able to put information into a concise, exciting, colorful, readable form better than a trained professional writer like you. So use the gems he gives you, but remember that you'll find most of them in piles of raw wordage that you have to refine. That's what you get paid for.

Did He Really Say That?

Talk is cheap. The people you interview can talk all day, and sometimes do. But you as a writer are limited. You have to say a lot in a few words. You can't waste words, and you can't afford to quote somebody who is wasting words.

So unless there could be some serious consequence of your editing, such as the Third World War or a messy divorce, be prepared to omit needless words from your quotes. When you're conducting an interview, most of the words you take down will prove unnecessary.

For example, if you ask the outgoing mayor what was the most exciting event in his forty-year political career, he's likely to say something like:

"Oh, gee, I don't know. There's been so much. It's all been exciting, really. I remember my brother Ralph one time telling me how much he envied my life in politics, for all the excitement. I mean, every two years your job is up for grabs; it's a real crap shoot. But the most exciting, huh? Oh, I don't know. Had a lot of excitement around here the day Councilman O'Meara left a bag of cash in the men's room. But you can't print that. The police strike of 1972. I guess maybe you could say that was the most exciting thing.''

The mayor's recollection of the most exciting event is just not worth that many printed words, so when you write it, it will come out like this:

"It's all been exciting,'' says Mayor Forbes, ''but the police strike of 1972 was the most exciting event.''

The quote works because it is the simple and complete answer to the question. Interviewees ramble; writers should not.

Throwing out the excess wordage is not the only kind of alteration you'll make in the interviews you conduct. You'll also be putting words into people's mouths so that you can include the question.

When I asked author James Carroll how he felt about the prospect of getting lots of money now that he had written a bestseller, *Mortal Friends*, he said, ''It has a kind of nonexistent quality for me. It doesn't mean much except that I can be secure for a couple of years and I can write what I want.''

If I had quoted *exactly* what he said, the reader would not know what "it" was, because Carroll was responding to a question the reader had not heard.

I could have used the reliable, but dull, ''When asked about the prospect of getting lots of money now that he's written a bestseller, James Carroll said . . . ''

But who wants to read an article in which every paragraph begins "When asked about . . . ?"

Not me.

Instead, I changed "it" to "the money." No harm done. Carroll's intent is intact, and the meaning is clear.

Don't be afraid to edit the spoken word. The fact that somebody said it does not mean you can't write it up in a forceful and interesting, if somewhat altered, manner. You have an obligation to the reader to provide him with good writing. And you have an obligation to your subject to write *only* things that he said, but not *everything* that he said. You should change words, but not meanings, and always ask yourself if the person you're quoting would have said it that way, given the opportunity.

What Dialogue Is

Dialogue, according to my dictionary, is "a conversation between two or more people." But in fiction writing the term is used more generally to mean the words a character speaks, whether he is with one or more people or alone.

Dialogue is the chocolate-covered munchies of fiction reading. Well-written dialogue is just a little more fun than the rest of writing. Dialogue, like nonfiction quotes, brings the people front and center.

What Dialogue Isn't

"Hi."

"Hi there. Just in time. I'm making pork chops."

"Good, I'll just wash up. Be with you in a sec."

"Did you pick up any milk at the store?"

"Yeah, but I had to get the half gallons. They didn't have any gallon jugs."

"That's okay."

"I got some bread, too."

"Whole wheat, I hope?"

"Sure."

Does this dialogue sound real?

It should. It's a transcript of a real conversation.

Is it good dialogue?

No. It provides very little information, tells you nothing about the characters, is as tension-free as an empty hammock, and is about as exciting as a three-week vacation in Elgin, Illinois.

Why?

Because dialogue that simply duplicates real speech doesn't work. When real people get together they say real dull things like, "Hi, how are you?" and "I'm fine, how's yourself?" and "See you later, I'm on my way to the store to pick up some cat food." Zzz.

"Hi, how are you?" isn't so bad when taken in the context of an entire relationship. Spoken words are usually accompanied by a smile, or sexual attraction, or friendship, or good memories about the time you and the speaker went to the ball game together. They also come with tone of voice; maybe a handshake or a hug. They are surrounded by visual stimuli. Often you can listen to them while getting other things done, such as picking your teeth, washing your canary, or opening a can of wax beans.

Little black lines on white paper have none of these things going for them. They have to be interesting all by themselves. They have to be a whole lot better than conversation.

So dialogue is not real speech. It only sounds like it.

When Should You Use Dialogue?

I once read that 20 percent of a story or novel should be dialogue. Twenty percent is a nice figure.

So is 7 percent. And 82 percent. They're all nice figures.

The fact is that some stories contain no dialogue. Others are 90 percent dialogue. Plays, of course, are nothing but dialogue. There is no right amount, and I can't give you any formula for distributing dialogue throughout your story.

But I *can* give you some general "when to use dialogue" tips, and if you combine these with an ear that's attuned to the rhythms of words and the overall pace of the story, you'll learn to put dialogue where it will work and omit it where it won't.

As with quotes, you use dialogue when you can provoke, humor, color, characterize, and stir an emotion better with a character's words than you can with your own. (That happens with dialogue much more often than with quotes, of course, because you're not limited to what somebody really said.)

Use dialogue when you want to break up long blocks of print.

I don't mean just turn any old bit of narrative into dialogue, but remember that the reader gets hungry for the sight and sound of dialogue. Find the best opportunity to satisfy his appetite.

Use dialogue when you're taking the reader on a long trip and he's going to need rest stops.

Sometimes in writing fiction it's necessary to cover a lot of space and time in a few pages. Your wagon train is moving through the Rockies during the hard winter of '84, and the reader is getting a bit weary of pain, and deprivation, and snow, and horses collapsing from exposure. Give the reader a break with a little dialogue that is stimulating, maybe even humorous. It will make him feel as if he's stopped and camped for the night, and he'll be rested for the next paragraphs between here and California.

Perhaps the most important *when* I can give you is this: Use dialogue when there is tension between your characters.

For example, if, as I did, you need the owner of several dress shops to walk into one store and tell his manager that he wants her to manage his new boutique in a remote resort town, he might say "Maggie, I'm giving you the Quishnook store to manage."

If she thinks that's a nifty idea and says "Thanks, Larry, that's sweet of you," and you continue with the story, there's no tension, and the dialogue really served no purpose. It was an annoying interruption—not a part of the movie, but more like someone talking in the theater. You could just as easily and effectively have written "Larry came in one day and told Maggie he was giving her the Quishnook store to manage. She thought that was a great idea and she thanked him."

On the other hand, if she doesn't want to manage the Quishnook store, there is tension. The issue is grounds for conflict between them, and if he comes in and says "I'm giving you the Quishnook store to manage," and she says "In a pig's eye!" and he says "What's the problem?" and she says "You know bloody well what the problem is," and he says "Try telling me. It will make things ever so much clearer," then you're off and running with some lively dialogue that moves the story along, provides information, and reveals character, even if she ends up going to Quishnook. (Which she does.)

Tension

Good dialogue between characters usually has an element of tension.

The tension I'm talking about is not just the obvious tension that is present when two people are arguing and you're wondering who's going to punch whom in the face. I'm talking about the tension that arises when the speakers are on the same side, but one is in conflict with himself, such as a young man trying to get up the nerve to ask for a kiss. There is tension in a dialogue between two people who love each other, but one doesn't know how to say it. The speakers don't have to be adversaries; there just needs to be some issue, some question, some sort of space between them that keeps the reader asking "What's he going to say now that she's said that?"

The reader should never have the sense that the speaker knew a half hour ago what he was going to say. Dialogue works best when it appears to be created at the moment, in response to the last words spoken. When you have two people speaking to each other, visualize each line of dialogue as having a hook on it that yanks out the next line of dialogue from the other character.

Here are two excerpts from recently published novels. In the first, from Dan Greenburg's *Love Kills* (Harcourt Brace Jovanovich, 1978), the two characters are not fighting, but they are in an adversary relationship. In the second excerpt, from Brian Garfield's *Wild Times* (Simon & Schuster, 1978), the two characters are on the same side; they care about each other. But notice that the tension is there in both excerpts, and notice that the lines of dialogue hook into each other. Dialogue is not just two monologues interrupting each other; it is a conversation in which each speaker's words are not determined until he has heard what the other has to say.

From *Love Kills:*

Max melodramatically takes out a pair of handcuffs and unlocks them.

"Now, then," says Max. "Are you still sticking to your story or aren't you?"

The formerly feisty doorman regards the cuffs thoughtfully and sighs.

"Ok. So I lied," he says.

"Oh, terrific. 'So I lied.' That's marvelous, absolutely marvelous. So because you lied we've been spinning our wheels while some maniac is out killing more women like Linda Lowry. You heard about the Rachlin case? The social worker on the West side?"

The doorman nods.

"That was probably the work of your delivery boy. Thanks to you he's going to have time for a few more free shots like that before we get him."

"Oh, take it easy. You want to hear my story or don't you?"

"Tell me your story, McMartin. Tell me why you lied to an officer of the law and withheld evidence and obstructed justice. I want to hear about that, you asshole."

"You call me asshole and you don't get my story."

"I don't get your story and I'm taking you in and booking you, and letting you spend a while in the slammer, explaining to your fellow prisoners why it is that all sex killers are boogies."

The doorman sighs a gigantic put-upon sigh.

"OK, McMartin, I'm all ears. Tell me about the delivery boy. What did he look like? What was he wearing? What was he delivering?"

"I didn't get that good a look at him, to be honest with ya. He was wearing a dark overcoat. And he wasn't no boy—he was maybe in his late thirties, and he was delivering flowers that said the name of the florist. East Side florists, or East River florists. Something like that."

"How tall was he? How heavy? What color was his hair? What color were his eyes?"

"I don't know. I have to be honest with ya. He was probably about average height. and I don't know if he was heavy. Maybe a little. And he was dark. Dark hair. And he had these sort of peculiar eyes."

Before we go on to *Wild Times*, I want you to note a couple of other things besides tension in Greenburg's dialogue while it's fresh in your mind.

First of all, I didn't have to set the scene for you. Greenburg writes his dialogue in such a way that you get caught up in the situation right off and have a pretty good idea of what's going on. The dialogue packs a lot of information.

Also, notice how rarely Greenburg tells you who is speaking. But you always know because of the words spoken, the speaker's relationship to the issue, and the speech patterns. Try to make your dialogue specific to the character; write words that only he would say.

Here is a bit of dialogue that has a different kind of tension running through it. The two people in the scene love each other, but because most people have difficulty in talking about their emotions, tension arises when they try to speak about love, anger, jealousy.

From *Wild Times:*

"We don't have much chance to talk, just the two of us."

"No ma'am."

"I'd been hoping by this time some of your reticence might have worn off."

"I'm not sure what you mean by that, ma'am."

"You keep to yourself too much, Hugh. You don't let anyone get close to you. Do you think that's fair?"

"I never meant to give offense, ma'am. I'm sorry."

"Sit on the step if you're a mind to—you don't need to stand there like a common hand with his hat in his hand." The rocker began to creak as Mrs. Tyree swayed gently back and fro. "I wish I knew what you were so afraid of."

"I don't guess I'm afraid of anything, Mrs. Tyree."

"Then why do you keep your distance so?"

"I am obliged for the things you've done for me, ma'am, but there's no way I can ever pay you back for them. I expect I don't feel too good about that."

"Poor Hugh. Is that it—are you trying not to increase your debt to us any more than you must?"

"Maybe something like that."

"Put it right out of your mind, then. Whatever we've done for you we've done because we wanted to, not because we felt we had to. No one's kept ledgers on you.''

"You've fed me and bought me clothes, given me saddle and horse, schooled me. . . .''

"And you've worked like a beaver to earn them. It's not as if we'd been supporting a shiftless lazybones, is it? Be fair to yourself. Who's put the meat on our table for the past three years?''

"Just the same, ma'am—''

"All we ask is your love, Hugh, but it's the one thing you've reserved from us. I find this very awkward but it must be said. We would appreciate some sign of your affection. You're always courteous, and always cool. I find it painful sometimes. You're such a good close friend to Kevin—can't you be a friend to his parents as well?''

Her words seemed to break something down inside me. I found myself crossing the veranda and picking up her hand. I had a frog in my throat and had to stop to clear it. "I'm sorry, ma'am, I never meant to do hurt. You've made a wonderful home for me here. I'll try to do better, I promise.''

I saw the moisture in her eyes before she averted her face. "It's all we ask.''

Milk the Dialogue

Tension works only if its end is delayed. You have to get the reader on edge and hold him there. So when your dialogue has grabbed him, got him wondering what's going to be said next, don't let him go quickly. Hold that interest by milking the dialogue, pulling it tighter and tighter. Remember, I'm not talking just about life-and-death situations; I'm talking about the everyday tensions that strain relationships between people.

Remember that scene with the boss trying to get Maggie to manage the dress shop in Quishnook? After six or seven lines of dialogue, they had hardly begun to fight. I milked it for all it was worth:

"Try telling me," Larry said. "It will make things ever so much clearer."

"This is not a major surprise," I said. [Maggie is telling the story.] "I've seen it coming ever since you bought that ridiculous little store. All you've talked about since February is how you've got to have the right person to manage the store and get your master plan off to a good start, how you're going to have a boutique in every resort town in the world."

"I've done all right so far."

"Yes," I said, "well, all that ambition is getting a bit tedious."

"You'll like Quishnook," Larry said. "Plenty of sunshine and the beach. You do look a bit pale."

"Pale, indeed! There's something seriously wrong with your mind if you think I'd give up my apartment and friends to spend a summer in some town nobody but you and God ever heard of."

Larry grabbed at his papers, shuffling them impatiently until he came up with an old issue of *Holiday* magazine. He flipped it open to a color layout on Quishnook, Massachusetts.

"Nobody ever heard of it, huh? What's this?"

"Okay, so a photographer from *Holiday* got off at the wrong bus stop once," I said. "What does that prove? I'm telling you the town is practically anonymous."

Larry smiled. "I realize, Margaret, that you don't know too much about business, but I thought you might understand that one key to business success is getting to things *before* everybody's heard of them."

"The point is moot," I said. "I'm not going."

"It's perfect for you in your condition. Plenty of fresh air.

I've rented you a cottage that's near everything.''

"Larry, the town is only three miles wide. *Everything* is near everything. And what exactly do you mean by my 'condition'?''

After this there is still more tension. The insults start to get personal. Each begins to dig into a stance from which he cannot move without losing face. Finally Larry threatens to fire her. She threatens to quit, and walks out of the store for her coffee break. A break in the tension, a breather. But even now the tension of the dialogue is helping the writing to work better, because all through the next scene the reader will keep reading to see who's going to say what when Maggie gets back.

Milk the dialogue. Don't end it too soon.

Movement

Dialogue is an integral part of your story, not an addition to it. Characters don't step forward and make speeches. Their words and actions are all part of the continuing flow of the story. You fold dialogue into narrative just as you fold egg whites into cake batter. They become inseparable.

Your dialogue works when it doesn't look like a chunk of writing that you jammed in between two paragraphs. To create this sense of movement, of a continuous flow of action, you inject movement, even unnecessary movement, into the dialogue itself. Just as actors on a stage rarely sit still and talk to each other, your characters should have some "business" to do when they talk, something to keep the story visually interesting. But, because dialogue must be fast-paced to work well, the action within it should move quickly. Include bits of description and action, but always get back to the words people are speaking.

In this scene from my book *The Pie-In-The-Face Murders*,

you'll see that none of the action is necessary to provide the information I want to get across, but the little bits of business make the dialogue more interesting. That, of course, is not the only job they do. These bits of business also reveal character, increase conflict, and make entire scenes more memorable to the reader. But they are especially efficient at improving dialogue. One reason is that they heighten the tension a little by making the reader wait an extra few seconds to hear "what he's going to say, now that the other fellow said that."

I left my truck parked in front of Frances Parang's house and walked to the service station. People get a little skeptical about my being a big-time magazine writer when they see me pull up in a laundry truck.

I found Galdetto in mortal combat with a soda machine that had screwed him out of a quarter. He was a big fellow, bright with sweat and bent like a bow because an enormous ball of flab hung from his middle like a sack of something heavy. He looked like the kind of guy who would throw a beer bottle at an umpire.

"Jerry Galdetto?" I asked.

"Yeah, yeah, who you picking?"

He didn't look at me. He looked straight at the soda machine as if it might jump him if he took his eyes off it.

"Nobody," I said. "Just want to ask you something."

"Yeah, well let me ask you something, what do you know about soccer, huh?" He pounded one of his beefy hands into the machine and waited for it to take a swing at him.

"Kyle Rote, Jr.," I said.

"What about him?"

"Nothing. I've heard of him, that's all. And that's all I know about soccer. Why?"

"Some guy wanted to place a soccer bet with me today. What do I know from soccer? Ain't that the game where they kick each other?"

"Something like that," I said. "They play it a lot in Europe who do you think killed Parang?"

"Shit, man, is that what you're here about?"

He turned and looked at me, then turned back quickly before the machine could find an opening. He jabbed it with his left hand. "Come on you animal," he screamed.

"You ain't a cop," he said. "You must be a reporter."

"Right."

"Well, I ain't saying nothing. I mean I know who killed Ace, there ain't no question about it. You think I don't know? I know all right. But I ain't saying nothing. When the time comes I'll take care of it for Ace, but other than that I ain't saying nothing about it. Come on, you motherfucking machine!"

"How about why?"

"How about why, what?"

"How about telling me why somebody had Parang killed?"

"You think I don't know, huh? I'll tell you why. Ace was blackmailing the guy, that's why. The guy come into some money and Ace figured he should get some."

"I see," I said. "It's all very clear now. Just some stranger Ace heard had money, some guy off the street, or maybe some guy he met at a Knights of Columbus meeting."

"No, pal, I ain't saying that. Don't you get what I'm saying? Ace was into something with the guy. The guy was supplying Ace with grass for a while, but he quit Ace a while back."

"Why?"

"He just finked out and said he wasn't interested no more. Only Ace found out the guy was coming into some money and was trying to protect himself. So Ace figured he was entitled to some of it. In return, he wasn't going to tell the police that this guy was supplying half the city with grass. Now that makes sense, don't it?''

"Sure. What was the guy's name?''

"You think I don't know?'' He punched the machine one last time, then said, "Aw the hell with it!'' He shoved another quarter into the slot and pressed the button. This time the soda came out.

"To tell you the truth,'' Galdetto said, "I don't actually know the guy's name. I never met him or nothing. But there's ways of finding out, you know.''

"I wish I knew some,'' I said.

If I had taken out that soda machine and just left in the words people spoke you would know a lot less about Galdetto, and the dialogue would not have worked as well. You'd find it hard to believe that Galdetto would stand around answering questions if he didn't have to stay in one place to get his soda. Also, the soda machine was something to "look at.'' Just as most people prefer television drama to radio drama, readers like to have something to "watch'' while they're listening to dialogue.

Don't Be Afraid to Say "He Said"

"I've got to go,'' she insisted.

"Then go,'' I responded, "but don't blame me if the ping-pong table gets warped.''

"Warped?'' she questioned. "But you promised . . . ''

"Promised?'' I challenged. "Promised, indeed! Men like me don't make promises.''

"Men like you!'' she exclaimed. "All men are like you: beastly!''

"Beastly?'' I sniffed. "You dare to call me beastly?''

"Yes, beastly,'' she intoned.

"Then go," I cautioned, "but don't walk down any dark alleys if you value your life."

The problem with that dialogue, aside from the fact that it's just some silly stuff I made up for fun, is that people are insisting, intoning, cautioning, responding, questioning, and challenging, but nobody seems to be *saying* anything.

Many beginning writers seem to cherish these synonyms for *say* or *said*, and they avoid "he said" and "she said" as if the phrases were carrying a fatal disease.

I think there are two reasons for this.

One is that the new writer is afraid of repeating the same word over and over. And well he should be. A word too often repeated reminds the reader that a writer is at work. But phrases like "he said," "she said," and "Hermonodo said" are an exception. Coming as they do on the coattails of dialogue, where the reader already knows that words are being said, the words *say* and *said* slip by unnoticed, while *sniffed*, *exclaimed*, and *orated* attract attention. The important thing is the noun or pronoun, the *he* or *she* or *Hermonodo* that lets the reader know who is speaking, and in good dialogue even most of those words are unnecessary. So limit the sniffs and the exclamations to those times when they really improve the writing in exchange for the small disturbance they cause. Use "he said" and "she said" and "the potato farmer said" to establish who is speaking, and return to them not with every exchange, but whenever there is a chance of the reader being uncertain about who is speaking.

Another reason many new writers use so many synonyms for *said* is that they don't think the words within the quotation marks convey the emotion or attitude they are trying to get across, so they try to bolster the statement by adding "he screamed" or "she persisted."

For the same reason, many also form the habit of tacking on adverbs to describe how something was said. Consider this:

"Go to hell!" he said angrily.

"I don't want to go to hell. I thought Miami Beach was too hot," he replied humorously.

"You know, you're really getting on my nerves," he shot back impatiently.

"I'm sorry. I'm usually more cheerful when people tell me I'm out on the street after forty years with a company," he said sarcastically.

"Okay, okay. Look, Dan, it's over. There's nothing more we can say to each other. Let's just end it," he sighed resignedly.

Now reread that dialogue and see if you can comprehend the tones and attitudes without any of the *-ly* adverbs. I'll bet you can.

There are exceptions, but generally dialogue that works is dialogue that clearly communicates the feelings and intentions of the speaker without being boosted by synonyms for *said* or adverbs such as *angrily* or *sadly*.

Don't underestimate the ability of the reader to catch the subtleties of speech. If you work hard at the dialogue and it sounds right to you, have faith that the reader, given the overall situation and the nature of the characters, will hear it as he should.

Dialogue Delivers Information

The reader gets many facts from dialogue, either because only the speaker knows the facts, or because the writer has concluded that dialogue is the most readable way to provide those facts.

But writing dialogue to provide information must be done with care. If it's obvious to the reader that dialogue is there only to provide information, he will feel as if he's been accosted in the middle of reading and told, "Just a minute, I've got to tell you some stuff you need to know before you read any further.'' This sort of dialogue is called *heavy-handed dialogue*, and it doesn't work. Heavy-handed dialogue results from characters speaking for the reader when they should be speaking for each other. George tells Joyce things that Joyce obviously already knows, and the reader loses the illusion that the conversation would take place even if he were not there to hear it.

Here are some facts that a writer needs to get across to the reader through dialogue:

A couple is waiting for a new car to be delivered. The car is a Mustang. The day is Saturday. It's raining out. Carolyn is the couple's daughter. Carolyn was recently in an automobile accident. The husband has to leave for Cincinnati the next day.

What these facts have in common is that the husband and wife already know them, and would not ordinarily tell them to each other. But you want to inform the reader of these facts through dialogue, so you have to work them in somehow.

Heavy-handed dialogue would go something like this:

"Gee, Joyce, do you suppose our brand-new red Mustang will be here soon? It's two o'clock, the time they promised delivery."

"Yes, George, today is Saturday. Another rainy Saturday!"

"I hope it gets here soon."

"Yes, it would be a shame if you didn't get to drive it today, since you've got to go to Cincinnati on business tomorrow."

"Well, if it doesn't show up until Monday, you make sure our daughter Carolyn doesn't drive it. I mean, after all, she had an automobile accident just last week."

Dialogue sounds phony when people tell each other things they already know. But dialogue that delivers information already known by the characters *will* work if you push the information into the background. Focus the sentences on something else.

"Well, it's two o'clock. Where's the car?"

"It will be here, George, just settle down. Today's Saturday—they're probably shorthanded."

"Shorthanded, hah! Probably joyriding in my car. They'd just better watch the cornering in this rain; I don't want to see a scratch on that car."

"Cornering? For God's sake, it's only a Mustang, it's not a Maserati."

"Yeah, well, it's *my* Mustang, and it looks like I'm not even going to get to drive it."

"You'll drive it, George, you'll drive it. Unless you're planning to stay in Cincinnati forever. Besides, you're not even leaving until tomorrow."

"They're probably picking up broads in it, that's what they're doing, picking up broads in my car. Look, if it doesn't show up until Monday, you guard it with your life. I don't want Carolyn near it, you understand. She is not to drive that car ever."

"Joanie Davis lets her daughter drive their new car."

"Joanie Davis's daughter didn't rack up our station wagon last Friday night."

"Oh, for crying out loud! Carolyn hit the ice and skidded. Could have happened to anybody."

Heavy-handed dialogue also occurs when one character tells another all kinds of things he didn't ask for, for no apparent reason except that the writer couldn't find a better place to provide the reader with the information. Consider this:

She responded just the way the women in his dreams had, pressing her body against his, clutching him with wild need, her heart pounding against his chest. Her lips turned to fire against his and he knew she wanted him more than she'd ever wanted anything.

"It's been so long," Don said. "Too long."

"Oh, it's been a long time for me, too," she murmured. "Ever since my husband drowned three years ago in a vat of chocolate syrup. He'd forgotten his life jacket. He was already dead when I got there. All this time I've wanted a man so badly, but I didn't dare. Even when I took that three-week vacation in Elgin, Illinois, I didn't fool around, though I had offers, believe me, lots of them. And at the rope factory, where I worked with my brother Dwight, there were lots of nice guys, but . . . "

Et cetera.

If you find yourself writing dialogue where people answer questions that weren't asked, then find some way of getting the question asked.

"How long's it been?"

"Five years. Ever since my husband died."

"Died? Aren't you a little young to be a widow?"

"He drowned. A vat of syrup and one careless step. That's all it took, and Hubie was gone. He was dead when I got there."

"Five years, and you've never been tempted?"

"Oh, I've been tempted all right. Couple of years back I spent three weeks in Elgin, Illinois. Quite a town, I'll tell you. Came close there, came real close."

"What stopped you?"

"Oh, I don't know. I was afraid I'd get a rep at the rope factory. Used to work there with my brother Dwight. There were a lot of nice guys there, too, and they weren't shy about asking, if you know what I mean. But . . ."

Using Dialogue to Characterize

When I talked about characterization, I said that the best tool you have is the words people speak. In your articles, quotes wisely chosen tell reams about the people who speak them. Remember Dolly Parton? In fiction, dialogue that is carefully crafted can be just as revealing of character. The words a character speaks reveal things about him in three ways: what he says, how he says it, and the fact that he said it.

For example, what if a man stands up in the middle of a wedding ceremony and shouts, "I ain't gonna listen to this crap no more"?

What he said reveals that he is dissatisfied, perhaps angry.

How he said it suggests that he is undereducated, and perhaps not too bright.

And the fact that he said it indicates that he is rude.

If he had turned instead to the person sitting next to him and quietly said, "I refuse to tolerate this poppycock any longer," he would have been characterized differently.

There's no point in my inventing bits of dialogue to show you that it can characterize. I've given many examples throughout this section. They weren't put there for that reason, but the fact is that when you write dialogue you almost can't avoid characterizing the speaker. You have observed character through dialogue if:

You thought Maggie was headstrong when she said, "In a pig's eye!"

You thought Larry was sarcastic when he said, "Try telling me. It will make things ever so much clearer."

You thought Hugh was proud when he said, "I am obliged for the things you've done for me, ma'am, but there's no way I can ever pay you back for them. I expect I don't feel too good about that."

You thought Galdetto was uncouth and dangerous when he

said, "Well I ain't saying nothing. I mean, I know who killed Ace, there ain't no question about it. You think I don't know? Shit, I know all right. But I ain't saying nothing. When the time comes I'll take care of it for Ace, but other than that I ain't saying nothing about it."

If you drew any conclusions at all about the characters because of what they said, then you've seen how quotes and dialogue reveal character. A character on paper emerges as a real live person for the reader through what he says, how he says it, and the fact that he says it.

Listen

I've tried to give you a lot of hints about using quotes and dialogue. That's the most any teacher can do. I can't tell you exactly what words to use. I can't give you a list of words that occur in speech and say that the ones in Column A will provoke, characterize, entertain, and the ones in Column B won't.

You'll have to listen for these things yourself. Everywhere. Eavesdrop shamelessly. Listen intently when people speak to you. Ask questions. Listen to the dialogue you read. Listen to yourself when you speak.

You should be listening for the words that carry the speaker's meaning and emotion. Spoken words are cheaper than salt, and most people use hundreds to get across a basic thought that can fit in six. Your job is to find those six words and make them sound as if they were the only six words the speaker used. Listen to conversations. They come not just in individual words, but in waves of meaning and emotion. Is this person expressing jealousy now? What are the best words he is using to show jealousy? Did the pilot's last five hundred words basically say that pilots are mentally unstable? What is the overall meaning or emotion in a block of words? Capture that, and then distill it.

You should also listen for the patterns of speech that come

with different feelings. In "The Hidden Work of Words," I talked about the speech patterns in your narrative: varied sentence length, incomplete sentences, and so on. I also talked about associating patterns of sound with patterns of action. Both of these concepts apply to quotes and dialogue, and if you listen carefully you will hear them.

You don't have to find a pattern of sound to convey every emotion your characters feel. But often the speech pattern will be a valuable tool in showing those emotions.

For example, when someone is *very* angry with you, you know it because he wraps his hands around your throat and squeezes hard, or shouts, or tosses your electric guitar out a ninth-floor window. But when someone is just a little bit angry with you, you know it entirely because of sound. The words he uses. His tone of voice, and his patterns of speech that the brain recognizes from the last time somebody was angry. One technique that you could use to express someone's anger is a declining sentence length.

"Wilma, I will not discuss this with you any further [ten words]. I have gone as far as I can [eight words]. I have had it [four words]. No more. That's it. Period."

This of course is followed in real life by the smallest number of words: zero. The silent treatment.

Don't drive yourself crazy trying to count the number of words people use to express different emotions. Just listen to the patterns, and try to duplicate those patterns with your quotes and dialogue.

A Quoting Game

Here are some words spoken to me in interviews. Try to turn them into strong quotes by eliminating the extra words without changing the speaker's meaning.

1. "You know I had this feeling come over me that I just wanted to do awful things, to get up and maim that person for life. I

wanted to make him suffer, hurt him badly, so that he would feel, oh, I don't know . . . punished, I guess, for what he had done. I really had a strong need for revenge, if you see what I mean. I wanted to get even.''

2. ''I think competence is the most appealing quality in a man. It's the thing that turns me on. It's the thing I look for when I meet a man. Is he good at what he does? That's the sexy quality, that ability to do a thing well. And he knows it. He's confident about it; that's part of the exciting quality.''

3. ''I don't know if I could have gotten out. I don't know if I could have made it. I think they had one of those doors with a buzzer. You know the kind, where the guy checks to see who's there and he pushes a button that unlocks the door. It breaks a circuit or something, I think. Anyhow, I wasn't thinking about escaping. I was thinking about what lies I could tell. The counselor was okay, he was a pretty good guy. He let me smoke.''

4. ''We want to do our music. People come up to us at clubs and concerts and they have requests for all kinds of things. They ask for the Rolling Stones or jazz stuff, or other kinds of music that you just wouldn't believe, music that has nothing to do with us. Things we never even thought of doing. We want to do the music that we like, the music we believe in. If we can't do the music we believe in, then it's just not worth it. It's not worth it to do music we don't care about. We don't want to do music we don't believe in.''

5. ''There was, oh I don't know, maybe two hours or more of pounding on the wall, very loud, too. It made an awful racket, this pounding. And sometimes there was a noise on the floor, a kind of thumping. A lot of thumping and pounding, could scare the hell out of you. Sometimes you'll go by a room and see a shadow. Nothing real, nothing solid, you know, just a kind of shadow, but when you go back there's nothing there. Just nothing.''

A Dialogue Game

Here are several situations. Using dialogue only, and no more than six exchanges, try to convey the situation to the reader. You can write "he said" or "she said," but nothing else besides the spoken words. Try to avoid heavy-handed dialogue such as, "Imagine me, the director, trying to talk a big star like you out of stage fright."

I'll do the first one as an example.

1. A boss of security guards is trying to exercise authority over a recalcitrant employee.

2. An astronaut is trying at the last minute to get out of going to the moon.

3. A major stage star is having an attack of stage fright before the debut of a new show; her director is trying to get her to go on.

4. A woman is trying to get her incompetent male secretary to resign without hurting his feelings.

5. A priest is counseling a teenage boy who thinks he is a homosexual.

6. An author is trying to get her publisher to accept a new book idea.

7. A lawyer is having trouble bringing up the subject of payment with a new client.

8. A bookie is trying to bribe a ping-pong player into throwing a game.

You can make up several more and try them. Here's my version of the first one.

"Why aren't you wearing a necktie?" he asked.

"You don't need them with the summer uniforms."

"You're not wearing a summer uniform. You're wearing a winter uniform. Ties are regulation with the winter uniform."

"Yes, but I'm only wearing a winter uniform because they didn't have any summer uniforms left. It's a substitute.

Since there is no such thing as a necktie with the summer uniform, I don't have to replace it."

"Look, I don't make the rules. I just enforce them. If you wear a winter uniform you must wear a necktie. It's as simple as that. If I make an exception for you, pretty soon everybody will want to dress like a slob in here, and I won't have that. I make periodic inspections and I expect you men to be in full uniform at all times."

☕ ☕ ☕ ☕ ☕ ☕ ☕ ☕   # Coffee Break

Whenever you write something, you enter into a contract with the reader. He agrees to read your words, and you agree to entertain, instruct, inform, or otherwise present him with something of value. Implicit in what you write are certain promises and rules. As long as he is fairly informed of what the rules are and you don't change the rules in the middle of the game, the reader will accept any set of rules.

If you break your promises or violate your own rules, your writing won't work.

If you begin your article, "Hudson's Fran Pratt, along with a handful of other experts in the nation, stands at the precipice of the next great social movement in America," you are promising your reader that you will tell him about Fran Pratt and a movement of some importance. If it turns out that Pratt is promoting legislation that would require checker players to wear safety helmets, you have broken your promise. The reader will be disturbed (unless you are being intentionally funny).

Or let's say you write a story about a private detective named Fred Royal. In the last scene Fred is trapped on the roof of a bowling alley with six mobsters surrounding him. They are carrying a steel chain net to capture him in so they can take him back to their hideout and beat the truth out of him. But just as they are closing in, you write:

> Fortunately, during the summer of his twelfth year Fred had made the remarkable discovery that he could fly like an eagle. Just as the net was about to land on him he leaped off the roof and soared away. I'll fly back to Elgin, Illinois, he thought, and figure out what to do next.

You've never mentioned this unusual talent of Fred's before. In effect, you announced at the beginning of your story "One of the rules is that Fred is just a regular, normal human being." So when Fred flew off the roof you broke your own rule. You cheated the reader, and he is justifiably angry with you. Your writing did not work.

On the other hand, if you had announced at the start of your story that your character, whom we'll call Clark Kent, came from another planet and had the ability to fly, your reader would accept it when he did. It would be consistent with one of the rules announced at the beginning of the game. But remember, if you say that Clark Kent can fly, you are also promising that he'll fly in the story, or at least that his ability to fly will somehow be relevant.

The point of view you use in your story (we'll be discussing this in detail later) is also an announcement of one of the rules. When you use omniscient viewpoint, you are announcing "One of the rules is that we (author and reader) can enter anybody's head and have access to all the pertinent information which will affect the action of the story."

If one of your major characters comes along in the last chapter and says, "Oh, Priscilla, I knew about your past all along. It doesn't matter. I still love you," and the reader didn't know that the character knew about Priscilla's past, you have broken the rule. The reader feels cheated. Your writing won't work.

Your writing also won't work if you force your viewpoint character to make farfetched observations to spare you from breaking your viewpoint rule:

Holmes held the tiny grains of sand in the palm of his hand, and I could tell by the way his eyes shone that he knew the sand could only have come from Carson Beach in Boston, Massachusetts. Surely this proved that the Colonel could not have spent his entire life in a Paris home for consumptives, as he had claimed.

Any author who would write such a thing had better not walk down any dark alleys.

Part

SIX

Description That Works

Setting the Scene

When you set a table, you deliver a message about what's going to happen. If there are soup bowls, then it's safe for your guest to predict that soup will be served. If there are wineglasses, wine will probably be poured.

It's the same in writing stories, articles, books. What you describe, what you set before the reader, delivers a message. If it delivers the message you want delivered, the writing works. If it delivers a message you didn't intend, then the writing doesn't work. But description always delivers *some* message about characters, plot, attitudes, and other elements of your story.

There is no such thing as objective description.

For any given passage there is a plethora of details you could put in, but the ones you select, deliberately and judiciously, are the ones that guide the reader's imagination. They tell him what to think, what to feel.

If you mention the chandeliers, the oil paintings, and the Chippendales, the reader gets the message, Here is affluence. If you write about the dim light, the one bare wall, and the sparse furnishings, you might create a picture of despair. All of these could be in the same room; in mentioning certain items, what you are really saying is "This is what my viewpoint character is aware of in this room."

You choose what to show, and the reader knows it. The reader assumes those particular items are examples of a larger concept you are trying to get across. He assumes writer *intent*.

Take a young man and put him on a typical city street on a summer afternoon. If he's just fallen in love, he might skip down the street "smiling back at the happy faces of other pedestrians." He might listen to "the music of the city," and watch the cars "roll up and down the city street."

If he's just been dumped by his girlfriend, he might move "listlessly through the smog-shrouded city, gazing without thought into the gray eyes of other lonely pedestrians.'' He might be more aware of the ''harsh city noises'' and the ''ugly metal monsters spewing fumes into the air.''

Same city. Same day. Same young man.

The difference is his mood, and the bits of description you use to convey it.

Messages are delivered by those parts of the scenery you choose to show. A city is polluted whether a young man in it is in love or not, but if you write ''Romantic thoughts of Ann Marie danced in his head as he skipped through the bleak, smog-shrouded city,'' your writing will not work.

You may have heard somewhere that if there is a gun on the wall in Chapter 1 it should always be fired by the last chapter. That's not literally true, but the idea behind it is correct.

If there is a gun on the wall in Chapter 1, the reader should, by the end of the book, have some idea of why you mentioned it but didn't, for example, mention the color of the rug.

Maybe the gun will be used to shoot somebody in Chapter 7.

Maybe the gun is an expensive make, and you're trying to convey a sense of affluence.

Or maybe you're trying to characterize somebody as having a ''gun collector's mentality,'' or the gun is the only object a young woman has that belonged to her father, or the gun is covering a button on the wall that opens a secret door.

The gun certainly doesn't have to be fired, but there should be some reason why you put it there in fiction, or why you choose to mention it in nonfiction.

If you think you're hearing an echo, you're right. These are the same things I said about characterization. The process is the same. At some level the reader is always asking ''Why are you telling me this?'' and if he doesn't understand why, he'll create an answer or lose his bearings. In either case you lose his attention, and your writing doesn't work.

Apply the Rules of Style

If you recall, I promised that the rules of style presented in Part 2 would be useful throughout the book. Let's look at how they can be used to improve description.

Be specific. Take a moment to think, but don't think about a box. Now, don't think about a black box. Now, don't think about a black box with shiny silver hinges on one side and a bright red star painted on the top of it.

You'll find that the more specific that box gets, the harder it is for you not to think about it, because the picture is getting clearer. Being specific works. If I tell you I met my wife in Boston you can sort of see us. But if I tell you I bumped into her on the statehouse steps you are more likely to see us. I have given you a specific scene in which to place us. If I tell you she wore a red dress you can see her. If I tell you she wore a cranberry red velvet dress you can see her better.

Use active voice. Look frequently for the descriptive noun and give it some action to perform, instead of having it just sit there passively.

Instead of the passive "There was mucky black water all over the cellar floor," try the active "Mucky black water covered the cellar floor."

Instead of "The auditorium was filled with bright light for the television cameras," try "Bright light flooded the auditorium."

Instead of "Everything from her shoulders to her knees was covered by a green sack dress," try "A green sack dress hung like musty drapes from her shoulders to her knees."

Say things in a positive way. Instead of describing the way things are not, describe the way they are.

Change "There was no color to her cheeks," to "Her cheeks were pale."

Change "There was no change left in the piggy bank," to "The piggy bank was empty."

Show, don't tell. Instead of telling "The face of the house was chipped and scarred," show "It looked as if it had been recently stoned by an enraged mob."

Change "Veronica was a windbag" to "She spoke for hours but said nothing."

Remember, these are not absolute rules to be applied to every sentence you write. They are general rules about what will make your description work better.

Keep Description Short

Have you ever wondered why some of the highly touted classics, the allegedly great books of the ages, are often as dull as cold pancakes?

One reason is too much description. It wasn't too much description then, but it is now.

How's that, Gary?

Well, consider the kangaroo, for example. Let's say that in 1817 some schoolmarm from Scituate, Massachusetts, took a voyage to Australia and came back to write about her adventure. No doubt she would include the kangaroo in her story, and if she could write well, a lengthy description of a kangaroo could be quite fascinating. Not too many people in Scituate had seen a kangaroo, or even a picture of one, by 1817. The writing would have worked.

If a descendant of that woman went to Australia today and came back and turned out long descriptions of kangaroos, you wouldn't read them. You'd say, "What does she think I am, an idiot? I know what a kangaroo looks like."

In fact, just about everybody knows what a kangaroo looks like. They've seen them in zoos, in movies, and on "Wild Wild World of Animals." Just the word *kangaroo* is enough to describe a kangaroo.

Unless you are writing science fiction or telling tales from some exotic land, chances are the reader has seen one of everything you describe. He will not tolerate long descriptions of things he can already see. Imagine how you would describe an airplane to an African tribesman who had never seen one. Then imagine how much shorter your description would be if you tried to describe it to the average American.

The reader's brain holds an enormous catalog of pictures. He has seen an infinity of images on television, and in movies, photographs, and real life. He knows how a vast number of things function, how they relate to one another. You don't have to describe them all.

For example, let's take aviation again, because it has gone from the unknown to the commonplace during the past century. What if your story takes place at an airport and you want to set the scene by creating a picture of a busy airport before you put your characters into action. Fifty years ago you might have gone on for pages, describing a runway as a long strip of land that airplanes roll on before they fly, explaining that a stewardess is a woman who wears a particular type of uniform and serves coffee on the plane. And you might write a long description of the control tower, since nobody would have seen a hundred and twelve airport movies at that point.

Today you might begin the same story:

La Guardia at noon. Businessmen and harried stewardesses rushing for the gates. Airplanes, too many of them, lined up on the runways. Porters and hustlers and gypsy girls with cookies and flowers for sale all working the terminal while the public address system crackles with flight numbers and in locker 301 the contents of a black suitcase tick off the last seconds in the lives of thirteen people.

How are the stewardesses dressed?
What color are the airplanes?

Do the porters have uniforms on?

What's in the black suitcase?

You can answer these questions and dozens more without further description, because you've *seen* all these things, either in real life or on television.

Keep description short. Aim for that density I talked about earlier by using a few carefully chosen words. The reader already has most of the pictures. You're just telling him which ones to look at.

The preachment to work with images already in the readers' heads applies not just to readers in general, but also to specific groups of readers.

For example, if I had written an article about stock car racing for an auto magazine, I wouldn't have spent many words describing the general atmosphere of stock car races. That would have been commonplace to my readers, and they would have turned to the next article quickly.

But I didn't write my article for a car magazine. I wrote it for a weekly entertainment magazine, specifically for readers who had never gone to the stock car races, but might like to try it. My description goal, then, was to show what the regular fan takes for granted and to show it in terms the general public is familiar with. I wrote in part:

Stock car racing is an experience with a mood and texture all its own. A carnival atmosphere clings to the speedway, whether it's slick and modern or crumbling at the corners. The smell of hot dogs and candied apples rushes to meet you in the parking lot, and when you get inside you are greeted by the roar of anxious engines. A kind of sweet nostalgia rises up from the infield and latches on to the breeze sweeping through the bleachers. Grease and noise that would horrify you at home take on a poetic luster, and even if talk of hemispherical head engines and four-barrel carbs means nothing to you, you get caught up in the enthusiasm that other people are feeling about these things.

When you are describing things and places the reader has seen, keep description short by reminding him of the pictures he has on file.

When you are describing things and places the reader has not seen, keep description short by using pieces of the pictures he has on file to create new pictures.

Putting Description in Motion

Another shortcoming of those big blocks of description that so infatuated readers a century ago is that they're static. They just sit there. They don't move.

The writer shows you the sunset, and gives you a list of colors in the afternoon sky. Then he shows you the clouds, even tells you what animals they're shaped like. Then he sketches the trees in the foreground, specifies the color of the dirt, points out the assorted wildlife, and finally describes a pair of lovers snuggled down under one of those trees.

It's a photograph in words.

That was fine when people didn't have photographs. But today they not only have photographs, they have television and movies. They also have cars they can drive to thousands of places from which to view real life. They have movement. Their pictures move, and if you are going to capture reader attention your pictures have to move, too. So think of your description not as a photograph but as a motion picture.

Description that moves is description that works.

There are two ways you can set your description in motion. The first, which you can always do, is to put the description itself into action by using active verbs and pictures of movement. The second, which you can usually do, is to sprinkle the description throughout the action of the story.

Keep in mind that *motion* doesn't necessarily mean that something has moved from Point A to Point B. It means that things are *doing* something instead of *being* something.

First, here are some bits of static description, a photograph:

The house on Wiley Street was white stucco with a red clay roof, a clone of every other house on the street. There was a pair of newly planted Malaysian dwarf palms on the small square lawn. There was a stone owl in front of the door. The name under the doorbell was Frances Parang.

She was sixtyish and tanned. She wore bifocals.

Her laugh was hoarse.

The house was small. It looked like a very neat apartment. The living room was very colorful. On the sideboard there were bright ceramic pots and homemade hand-painted planters with plastic flowers in them. There were several lamps in the room.

There was also a bookcase.

Now here is some of that static description brought to life through the use of active verbs and motion pictures. A good key to getting your static description in motion is to look at the object you want to describe and ask yourself not "What is it?" but "What does it do?"

The house on Wiley Street was white stucco with a red clay roof, a clone of every other house on the street. A pair of newly planted Malaysian dwarf palms stood guard on the small square lawn, and a stone owl sat in front of the door. The name Frances Parang had been carefully printed under the doorbell.

She was sixtyish and tanned. Her bifocals twinkled at me as she tipped her head to get a better look.

She laughed a hoarse laugh.

The house felt smaller inside. It felt not like a house at all, but like an apartment where everything is neatly in place because the residents have nothing but housework to do. The living room was a crowd of colors, each battling for dominance. It was filled with bright ceramic pots on sideboards, homemade and hand-painted planters filled with plastic flowers, and things that dangled from the ceiling and tinkled when you walked by them. There were also enough lamps to illuminate a night baseball game.

Frances poured the wine while I fingered her bookcase.

And here is that static description brought to life and given forward motion by being sprinkled into the current as the action of the story flows by.

The house on Wiley Street was white stucco, with a red clay roof, a clone of every other house on the street. A pair of newly planted Malaysian dwarf palms stood guard on the small square lawn, and a stone owl sat in front of the door. The name Frances Parang had been carefully printed under the doorbell.

She came to the door and peered through the screen. She was sixtyish and tanned. Her bifocals twinkled at me as she tipped her head to get a better look.

"What do you want?" she said in a voice so husky you could almost hear the polyps knocking together.

"Hi, my name's Randy Chase."

"What do you want?"

"I'm a reporter for the *Scream*."

"Yeah, so what do you want?"

"I want to talk to you about your husband getting knocked off," I said. It was not a very tactful thing to say, but she just didn't strike me as the grieving widow.

She laughed a hoarse laugh. "You've got a lot of chutzpah saying a thing like that. The poor bastard's not even buried yet. You've sure got chutzpah. You know what chutzpah is, huh, do you know what chutzpah is?''

She seemed oddly familiar to me now. I was sure I'd had this conversation before.

"Something like balls, isn't it?''

Frances laughed again. "Yeah, that's what it is. Exactly. Balls! Come on in, you're okay." She pushed the screen door open and welcomed me into the shady coolness of her foyer.

"You want some wine?" she said. I followed her into the living room. "I was just having some. Nothing fancy, just some cherry crap Asa always had around. I drink it with ice."

The house felt smaller inside. It felt not like a house at all, but like an apartment where everything is neatly in place because the residents have nothing but housework to do. The living room was a crowd of colors, each battling for dominance. It was filled with bright ceramic pots on sideboards, homemade and hand-painted planters sprouting plastic flowers, and things that dangled from the ceiling and tinkled when you walked by them. There were also enough lamps to illuminate a night baseball game. While Frances poured the wine I fingered her bookcase.

Don't stop to admire the scenery. Reveal it through the action of the characters and the forward motion of the story. Think of the verbs. Have someone run his fingers over the books in the bookcase or sink into a cushioned wicker chair or lean over to sniff the roses in the vase. You'll not only tell the reader there's a bookcase, a wicker chair, and a vase of roses in the room, but you'll also give him something interesting to watch while you're doing it.

A Game to Put Description in Motion

Here is a list of environments and some of the things in them that you can use for description. With each one, try first to make the descriptions move by using active verbs, by making the things *do* something. Then try to make the description move before the reader's eyes by putting a character into the scene and revealing the objects through his actions. I'll do the first one as an example.

1. A church containing carpets, pews, and candles.
2. A poker game containing cigarettes, chips, and cards.
3. A library containing silence, books, and phonographs.
4. A hallway containing puddles, windows, and an elevator.
5. A house on the night before Christmas containing silence, stockings, and dreams.
6. A writer's study containing an electric typewriter, a waste-basket, and a phone.
7. An airport containing airplanes, a loudspeaker, and lockers.

For number one I asked myself first what my descriptive objects do. I decided that carpets can lie, line, or cover; candles can glow, stand, line, or shrink; and pews can fill, cover, crowd, or face. I decided to move my descriptive objects past the reader's eyes by writing "The carpets stretched all the way to the altar," "The candles glowed on both sides of the sanctuary," and "The rows of empty pews waited for the morning wor-shipers." When I put a person into the scene I wrote "He walked on the carpet." "He lit a candle." "He slipped into a pew."

You do the others. Some are quite difficult, but they will help you think of description as a motion picture instead of a photo-graph.

Use Details That Work

Every person, place, thing, or action that you describe will have many qualities, such as weight, color, texture, speed, thickness, sound, and temperature. You certainly don't have to rattle off a whole list of them to capture your reader. It takes very few words to create a picture if the words are chosen carefully.

If your goal were simply to show the reader a picture, you could describe the weight of an object, or its color, or its texture—almost any fairly vivid detail—and the reader would see it. But writing that works doesn't just show the reader a picture. It also gets him to look at it in a certain way.

For example, if I just want you to see the trousers that a man is wearing I could tell you their color (blue), the fabric they are made of (denim), or the price he paid for them. ("He came in wearing eighty-dollar jeans.") But description usually involves greater goals than that, and if I wanted you to look at the pants as an aspect of this man's sexuality, his attractiveness, the detail I choose might be *tight*. It doesn't take any more words to write "tight jeans" than it does to write "blue jeans" or "denim jeans." But I have gotten more for my words by choosing the detail that does the work I want it to do.

For another example, let's say that there's a car in your story. There are hundreds of details about that car, and you could use almost any one of them to show the car to your reader. Tell him it is a Chevrolet Monza and he will see it. Tell him it has a flat tire and he will see it. Tell him the hood is up and he will see it. The reader will extend the lines, just as he does with characters.

But when you write a story or article, you have more in mind than simply creating pictures. You want to plot, you want to characterize, you want to editorialize, you want to evoke feeling. Establish your goals, and then choose the descriptive details that will work toward those goals.

If your goal is to characterize the driver as reckless, you might describe the car as being "pitted with dents."

If you're trying to show a typical middle-class suburban family, you might mention that the car is a "station wagon."

If your piece concerns ecology or consumerism, the car might be a "gas guzzler."

If you're trying to be funny, the car might be a "pile of scrap metal on wheels."

Any one of these will show the reader a car, but each will get him to look at the car in a specific way, and that specific view is what reveals information about a character or situation.

Consider this:

A writer for the Bucks County (Pa.) *Courier-Times* goes to visit a young woman named Ann Melville. He wants to write an article on her adventures for the Sunday morning edition of the paper. He meets Ann. He sees what she looks like, her height, her clothing, her movements. He sees her house; he knows the color of the carpets, the kind of furniture, etc. He interviews her and finds out about her history of travel. By the time he leaves her house late in the afternoon, his head is full of details. He has checked to see if she wears any rings. He has scanned the dining room walls for photographs. He has listened for speech patterns.

With a head glutted with details, he'll have no problem finding *something* that will show you the young woman and her house and history. *His problem is to select the right descriptive details for the story he is writing.* So he asks himself "Am I writing 'The Life of Ann Melville'? No." So he decides not to mention her record collection and a dog she once loved. "Am I writing 'The Houses of Bucks County'? No." So he decides not to mention the shutters on the windows or the imported gravel in the driveway.

"What I'm writing," he decides, "is 'Young Woman Has Had Lots of Travel Adventures.' "

Now he knows what work he wants his descriptive details to do besides show pictures, so in an article that eventually got titled "Around the World with Edgely's Ann Melville," *Courier-Times* staff writer Jack Shandle began:

> Outward-bound, exotically innocent creatures like Ann Melville, young women whose eyes can at the same time

shine with wholesomeness and lust for adventure, always seem to be pestered in conversation by unruly wisps of hair that lope from their shoulders to seductively veil their faces.

They also share a certain offhand way of flipping the veil aside.

So it is with Ann, who has spent a good part of her twenty years touring Greece in donkey carts, spidering over the rigging of three-masted ships, and searching out troglodytes in Tunisia. Yet on a recent December day, shortly after learning what her newest adventure would be, she seemed at times like any average Bucks County Community College student pouring tea in the living room of her mother's Edgely home.

Only at times.

Light from the sun setting on the softly flowing Delaware streamed through the window. Screened by golden filaments of Ann's hair, it edged the semidarkness softly, suggesting other times, adventures, faraway lands. Yellow-bordered issues of *National Geographic* and *Geo* magazine that had been all but swallowed up in a confusion of correspondence on the coffee table added a substantial note to the mystique.

Can you see adventuresome Ann Melville's entire body and face even though Shandle only made reference to her eyes and hair?

Can you see her many and varied land travels even though the only transportation detail he used was "donkey carts"?

Can you see Ann working on those three-masted schooners because Shandle used a word like *spidering* that shows you her limbs and at the same time reminds you of ropes, nets, and perhaps even sails?

Can you envision all her adventures even though he only referred here to the search for troglodytes in Tunisia?

Can you see her at home because she is "pouring tea in the living room"?

Can you see how Ann's adventurous character has furnished the house with *National Geographic* and *Geo* magazines and that correspondence on the coffee table?

Can you see that all these carefully chosen details of description make you look at Ann the way the writer wants you to?

I've only given you the first few paragraphs, and already Shandle's got you convinced that you can see this young woman and that she is adventuresome. This was nonfiction, but the result would have been just the same in fiction.

Make description work by finding the details that do the job you want done.

Plants

If you pick up tomorrow morning's newspaper and find out that good old Tommy Slater, whom you went to high school with, stuck a pistol in his mouth and blew his head off last Thursday afternoon, you're likely to say something like "That's unbelievable, Tommy Slater committing suicide!"

On the other hand, if you had run into Tommy three weeks ago at the supermarket and he was really down because he'd just been fired, and then last week you'd heard Tommy was getting divorced, your reaction to the newspaper story might be something like "I'm not surprised. I saw it coming."

In either case, Tommy Slater is the same guy with the same history. But in the second case, the possibility of a Slater suicide had been planted in your brain, and you found it easier to believe when it happened.

In writing, you will often plant ideas in the reader's brain in order to make subsequent incidents believable. Readers will believe anything if it's consistent with information they've already got.

The job you want description to do in the case of plants is to firmly imprint on the reader's brain the information that will make an incident believable when he recalls it later.

In a story about Tommy Slater you might write "Tommy smoked constantly during the few minutes we talked at the supermarket. His gray eyes refused to focus on me, and the pale unshaven flesh on his cheeks hung like wrinkled sheets because he had dropped sixteen pounds since he'd gotten fired. 'I'm thirty-seven,' he told me. 'I don't know how to start all over.' "

Later on when you tell the reader that Tommy Slater committed suicide, he's going to remember the gray eyes and neglected appearance. The suicide is going to "fit in" with his information about Tommy Slater.

Plants are not just for people. If you refer to the "creaking every time we drove the old van over Crawford's Bridge," the reader will easily accept the fact later that half of Crawford's Bridge dropped into the bay, stranding your hero on an island in a storm.

In an article about a jailbreak, if you quote one of the guards in the fifth paragraph as saying "One of the pies seemed a little heavier than usual that day, but I didn't think much about it," your reader will find it easier to believe when the warden theorizes later in your article "I think I know how they got a gun. I think it was in one of the lemon meringue pies."

Tags

My friend Mack Mitchell is a minister who drives around in a sleek black sports car—a Jensen-Healey with a beige racing stripe. And I imagine that a lot of people explain who Mack is to other people by calling him "the minister who drives the black sports car." If they referred to him as "the minister who's got a teenaged daughter" or "the minister who lives over in Northboro," it wouldn't do any good because the description wouldn't separate him from other ministers. So unconsciously they find something that distinguishes Mack from all the other ministers in the listeners' mind: the black Jensen-Healey. Mack Mitchell wears a tag that says "black sports car" on it. If I need to remind you of who he is later on in this book, I will simply mention the car, and you will remember the person who goes with it.

A character tag such as Mack Mitchell's black Jensen-Healey is usually attached to a character the reader won't be seeing for a while. If a woman is being followed by a man in Chapter 2, and in Chapter 10 she steps onto an elevator and suddenly realizes she is with "the man who had followed her home from the bowling alley that morning in March," the reader will have trouble remembering that there had been a man following her earlier. But if you had given the man a limp, or a gleaming earring in his left ear, or a persistent cough, the reader will remember it vividly when he sees the limp or the earring or hears the cough again.

The same goes for places and objects. If you take your reader briefly to a summer cottage and tag it with "the cacophony of bullfrogs croaking all night long," then later on when you refer to that sound the reader will remember the cottage.

The tags that work best are the ones that appeal strongly to the senses. A bright color, a sharp smell, a grating sound will all leave a vivid imprint on the reader's brain.

A tag must be distinctive. It doesn't do any good to have your woman followed by a man with bright red hair if you're going to have six other guys with bright red hair come into her life before she gets on the elevator.

Similes, Metaphors, Etc.

Beginning writers, particularly the ones who took business

courses in high school and skipped college, are often intimidated by those literary terms that clutter the pages of English textbooks but hardly ever come up in real life. Perhaps you trembled inside once or twice at a social gathering when some pseudointellectual began yammering about allegories and analogies, epigrams and aphorisms, similes and metaphors. You might even have wondered "How can I call myself a writer when I don't even know what this guy is talking about?"

Well, all of these are useful tools for the writer, and if you know the terms you'll feel more secure at cocktail parties. But it is more important to remember that writing is an art, and that great books are sometimes written by people who wouldn't know an aphorism if it landed in their soup. You don't have to know the terms to use the tools. You use them all the time.

I'm going to deal with two of them here just to show you that they are approachable. They don't bite. You'll see that you are already using them and they can make your writing work, or you can misuse them and your writing won't work.

First of all, a *simile* is a phrase that says something is like something else. It says that two things are similar, though usually in just one or two ways.

Some similes are used so often they've become clichés (remember them?):

"He was like a bull in a china shop." "She was like a volcano about to erupt."

You should stay away from these. Remember that clichés remind the reader that a writer is at work.

Similes are good descriptive tools that can make your writing more colorful, more interesting.

They can be used to make the abstract visual:

"The grief he felt was like a cold and jagged rock lodged in his heart."

They can be used to make the general specific:

"The subject of money is here again, waiting like a bellboy

with his hand out for a tip."

They can be used to strengthen other images through association:

"The boxer had a face like a fist."

Similes don't work when the images they create are so farfetched they are humorous:

"The drugged mouse lumbered like a confused elephant through the laboratory maze."

Similes also don't work when the two things being compared are too much alike:

"The gazelle was as graceful as a deer."

A lot of writers have a hard time distinguishing between a simile and a *metaphor*. I think the best way is to remember that there is no *like* in a metaphor. A simile says something is *like* something else. A metaphor says something *is* something else.

A metaphor can be a sentence, a paragraph, even an entire book. As long as you are pretending that a person or thing is another person or thing, you are continuing the metaphor.

Metaphors pop up everywhere in conversation.

We use our divisions of time metaphorically:

"It was the dawn of a new career." "They had come to the autumn of their years." "An eleventh-hour victory."

We use lots of sports metaphors:

"He spent the whole week looking for a job. He struck out on Tuesday, but hit a home run on Friday."

"There's nothing left to do but punt."

Metaphors are used for all of the reasons similes are used: to make the abstract visual, to make the general specific, to make the complex simple. For example, to describe a woman's recent success in business, you might simplify her activities through the metaphor of flight by saying "She soared above her peers and landed right on schedule in the president's office."

Metaphors, like similes, fail when they are too farfetched:

"With his children in jail and his wife in the arms of another man, Pernell was desperate. He was a planet hurtling toward destruction in some as yet unseen galaxy.''

And metaphors fail when they are too similar to what they are replacing:

"The mule, old and weary, was a thoroughbred that had run its last race. Never again would it hear the trumpet and streak around the track of life.''

This sort of metaphor confuses a reader because he can almost see it, and he doesn't know if he's supposed to or not. A mule is like a horse and could conceivably race around a track. On the other hand, the reader knows that people don't really hit home runs in employment offices.

Metaphors that are too farfetched or too close to reality don't work because they remind the reader that a writer is at work.

In learning to use metaphors, the beginning writer often stumbles onto the scene with something called the *mixed metaphor*.

It would be a mixed metaphor if, for example, the man who was job-hunting struck out on Tuesday and then scored a touchdown on Friday. The writer confuses his readers by first telling them that life is a baseball game and then changing his mind and saying, no, I was wrong. Life is really a football game.

How about a woman who's decided to take a chance on marrying a guy whose record is a little spotty:

"She rolled the dice and waited to see what happened. But there was always Stan, her ex-boyfriend, who was willing to take her away. He was the ace up her sleeve.''

Mixed metaphors don't work.

A Metaphor Game

Here is a list of subjects and metaphorical ways you might write about them. I'll do the first one as an example.

1. Death as a metaphor for a lost pennant.
2. Being a miner as a metaphor to show that writers really do work hard.

3. Escape from prison as a metaphor for women's liberation.
4. Military strategy as a metaphor for lovemaking.
5. A hurricane as a metaphor for a marriage in trouble.
   Here is how the first one might show up on the sports pages:

The Red Sox pennant hopes died suddenly yesterday afternoon at four o'clock. Death came when Yankee slugger Reggie Jackson launched a towering three-run homer into the centerfield bleachers. Jackson's sixth-inning blast gave the Yankees a seven-run lead, and from then on there was clearly no sign of a heartbeat in the pennant hopes, which had been critically ill since a nine-game losing streak in late August. The mourners came to the plate, Yastrzemski, Rice, Fisk, but there was not a twitch or a twitter from the corpse.

Funeral services were held at this morning's Fenway Park press conference, with manager Don Zimmer reading the eulogy. "We just didn't have the pitching," he said.

This year, with several key players nearing retirement age and few good prospects coming up, New England's pennant hopes will be buried just a little deeper than usual.

Part

SEVEN

Points of View

Sensory Viewpoint

Think about a house. It could be a house you once lived in, or one you've visited often, or one you've always wanted to own.

Now think about where you are in relation to that house. Are you in front of it? Behind it? Are you in the yard looking at the side of the house? Are you floating above it, looking down at the roof? Where are you?

Now imagine that you are not in front of the house. You are not behind it. You are not beside it or below it or above it. You are no place in relation to the house. Can you do it? Can you be no place in relation to the house and still see the house?

Of course not. You have to be someplace in relation to a thing in order to see it.

And your reader always has to be somewhere in relation to your writing in order to see it. That's his sensory viewpoint.

The sensory viewpoint is the place from which the reader views the action of your story or article. Because most writing is visual, viewpoint is usually discussed in visual terms. I am calling it *sensory* viewpoint because, obviously, the place from which the reader sees something is also the place from which he hears, smells, tastes, and touches something.

Your writing won't work if you don't have a clear concept of where your reader is standing in relation to the action of your story. Try to keep the reader in one place as much as possible, and when you do move him, do it smoothly, at appropriate times and for good reasons.

To get an idea of how your reader will feel if you switch viewpoint inappropriately and arbitrarily, imagine that you are reading a story in which the writer has led you to a modern ranch-style house on a suburban side street, and has described the front of it.

Then he writes:

Tony came out the front door clutching his briefcase as if

the secrets of the neutron bomb were in it. Helen was right behind him.

"Yes, Helen. Well, I've had just about enough of this," Tony said. He turned and faced her. He was almost close enough to bite her nose off.

"You have, huh?" she shouted. Tony winced. "Well, don't come back here," she said. "Bernard will be happy to take your place."

"Bernard?" Tony said. "Bernard!" His face turned the color of fresh raspberries. "Bernard," he cried once more, and he pulled open his briefcase. "You and Bernard will never see each other again." He reached into the briefcase.

Bernard was still in the living room with Linda.

"It's the story of the age," he said to her. "I mean, this will make my reputation as a journalist. I won't have to write columns about dog care anymore. I'll make millions."

"Look, Bernard, honey, I can't stand the suspense any longer," Linda said. "Will you tell me what it is?"

Bernard paused. "Well, you're not going to believe this," he said, "but I know what happened to Judge Crater and Amelia Earhart, and I've got proof."

"Proof? You've got proof? What, what? Tell me, before I burst!"

"Okay, I will. The whole story started coming to me when I was talking with Sturge Thibedeau. You know, the guy who's been working on the roof."

At that moment Sturge was up on the roof tugging a mysterious package out from between two loose bricks in the chimney. Once he had it in his hands he unwrapped it slowly. He was astonished at what he found inside.

Meanwhile, down in the cellar . . .

Do you see what's happening here? You're being yanked around and you don't like it. This, of course, is an extreme example to demonstrate what many writers do in a less obvious, but still jarring, way. You'll see when we discuss *omniscient viewpoint* that there are times when you will move your reader smoothly and logically from place to place, character to character. But don't yank your reader around unnecessarily, because he won't like it. Don't keep changing his sensory viewpoint.

Mental Viewpoint

If a suicidal old man stands on the ledge that juts out from the south wall of a canyon, he can look out over the canyon with at least two viewpoints. One is that sensory viewpoint we've been discussing. It allows him to see the bottom of the canyon and the north, west, and east walls. He cannot see the south wall because of where he stands, but it is the only wall he can touch. His sensory viewpoint is controlled by where his body, which houses his senses, is placed.

And because he is about to leap off the ledge, he has a special mental viewpoint of the canyon. He might see it as a symbol for the end of the world, salvation, a womb to which he is returning, or a dozen other things.

But let us imagine for a moment that he is not standing on the ledge. He's back home in Tucumcari deep in a suicidal funk, and he's thinking about finding a canyon somewhere to leap into. Now, as he starts to picture the canyon, he can see all four walls if he wants to. He can see the canyon in any way, from any angle, because the image is in his mind. But as he invents this canyon in his mind, his visual view of it will be greatly influenced by his depressed state, his mental view. Perhaps he sees it as much lighter or darker than any canyon could be. Perhaps it is bottomless. His sensory viewpoint and his mental viewpoint merge: they interact; they become a single, complex sensory-mental viewpoint.

Your reader is more like that man back home in Tucumcari than the one standing on the ledge. Two people standing on a ledge will see, hear, and touch pretty much the same thing. Two people reading about a canyon will not. They are looking at black lines on white paper, and each will make up a canyon of his own.

Each will dream it up in any way he wants that does not conflict with the information you have provided. His canyon will be sculpted by all the other elements of your story, all the canyons he's seen in life and on television, his mood of the moment, and whatever impinges upon his senses while he's reading your canyon scene. Sensory viewpoint and mental viewpoint become inseparable. They are ingredients in the same soup. That is why I have broadened my discussion of viewpoint to include aspects of mental viewpoint such as theme and slant.

Viewpoint Is Not Person

When you studied grammar in school, everything was divided into categories. Gender. Number. Case. And person. Person, you may recall, went like this:

First person: I, we.

Second person: you.

Third person: he, she, it, they.

The reason I mention this is that it's very easy for new writers to confuse the concepts of *person* and *viewpoint*. But they are two different things. I am the same *person* no matter where I go, but my viewpoint changes every time I change my position or mental attitude. This holds true whether you see me through myself or through someone writing about me.

So when you hear reference to "point-of-view character," it doesn't necessarily mean that the character is speaking in the first person.

"My name is Louise, and from here in my cottage I can see the Girl Scout camp across the pond" is a first-person sentence with Louise as the viewpoint character.

"Louise stood by the window in her cottage; across the pond she could see the Girl Scout camp" is a third-person sentence, but Louise is still the viewpoint character.

How Many Sensory Viewpoints Are There?

There are several established, classified viewpoints. You might meet one writer who talks about two of them. You might meet another writer who refers to seven. Each viewpoint is useful because it is like a pole in the desert: it gives you some sense of where you are in reference to where you began. It gives you a bearing from which to navigate. Actually, there is no set number of viewpoints. Each well-defined viewpoint is just one on what might be seen as a continuum of sensory viewpoint.

This is true because the reader has to use someone else's eyes, ears, nose, sense of touch. The reader is inside the head of a character or the author looking out, but he doesn't always know what influences are tainting that person's view of the scene.

There is an infinite number of objects and occurrences that can alter our perception of a scene, even if we don't budge from our viewpoint spot. And no two people, if they could stand in the same spot at the same time, would see exactly the same. The focus of each person differs.

Sensory viewpoint involves not just where the reader is standing, but how much information is revealed to him and how much is concealed from him.

That is why you and I could sit around making up new viewpoints all night. "How's this?" I could say. "My main character is a mind reader, but she doesn't have the power on Tuesdays. Only she doesn't know she doesn't have the power on Tuesdays. Tuesdays don't exist for her, and she's not aware of anything that happens on a Tuesday.''

Then you could come back with a minor character viewpoint in which the minor character has reason to hate the main character and might at any time be telling lies about him.

You can see where this business of sensory viewpoint blends with mental viewpoint. It's that soup again.

Having said all this, let me give you some examples of the established sensory viewpoints, so that you will have those bearings that will guide you as you navigate.

Omniscient viewpoint is the one in which the narrator knows all.

He can be inside each character's mind:

Carla wondered if he would kiss her, now that they had been out twenty-seven times. She stopped and checked her face in the store window.

Fred was unaware of her movements. He was contemplating the Jets-Colts game, wondering if he could get tickets.

The narrator can go anywhere:

Meanwhile, back in Elgin, Illinois, Carla's father was wondering what kind of trouble his daughter was getting into in the big city.

He can predict the future:

Little did Fred know that the Jets-Colts game would be the most boring contest in the history of sports.

Objective viewpoint is the one that newspaper stories are supposed to be written from. It presents only facts that are the same no matter who is writing them:

"The mayor slammed his fist down on the table.

" 'Dammit, I want those manhole covers renamed personhole covers,' he said. 'The women in this town vote.' "

That's objective. I told you what he did and what he said. If I had said he was angry it would not be objective, because somebody else might interpret his action as insistent, impatient, or whatever. If I said he wanted the manhole covers renamed out of expediency because he needed the female vote, that would not be objective. Someone else might say he's an ardent feminist, trying to do the right thing for the women of the town.

Character viewpoint is the most common viewpoint. With character viewpoint the reader hitches a ride in a character's head, usually the main character, and follows him throughout your story or article. The reader sees things through his eyes, hears things through his ears.

The reader in a sense *is* the character, and at any point the reader knows exactly as much as the character does. However, character viewpoint does not have to be objective. It can be prejudiced, hostile, and misinformed:

Larry heard the alarm. He rolled over and shut it off. It was six a.m. He turned back and looked at his wife. Her face looked like a squashed lemon. Ordinarily when he gazed at her in the morning her face would seem angelic. But ordinarily they wouldn't have spent the evening hollering at each other and threatening divorce. He couldn't stand to look at her, and he knew the anger was still in him.

From this point of view the reader can't be told what's happening in the other room, but he can be told "Larry heard some thumping from the kids' bedroom. It sounded as if they were conducting the Third World War on their beds."

The reader can't know that the governor died last night until Larry turns on the radio and hears it, or someone calls him up and tells him, or "He picked up the morning paper. 'Governor

Humwicker drowns in vat of chocolate syrup' screamed the headline.''

With character viewpoint the reader and the character see the story from the same place.

In a novel you might change from one character viewpoint to another many times, but that is not the same as omniscient viewpoint, because at any time the reader is limited to the information in the head of a single character. If your first chapter is from Larry's viewpoint, for example, and then your second chapter is from Marilyn's, you could not write in the second chapter ''Larry was sneaking up behind Marilyn with a hammer in his hand.''

The reader is supposed to be inside Marilyn's head, and Marilyn doesn't know Larry is there. But you could write ''Marilyn heard something behind her. She turned. There was Larry with a hammer in his hand.''

Why Use One Viewpoint Instead of Another?

Any story can be told from many different viewpoints. Some stories require that information be withheld from the reader for an effect. The most obvious example of that would be the murder mystery, in which the reader is given clues and the culprit is revealed at the end. In such a case you couldn't very well make the murderer the viewpoint character, because he would never wonder whodunit. If your character is going to die halfway through the story, then obviously he cannot be the viewpoint character either.

You have to decide who your story is about, and what information you want the reader to have at what point. The choice of viewpoint is not an arbitrary one; it influences every word, every incident in the story.

There is no better example of this than the Sherlock Holmes stories, which are told from the viewpoint of a secondary character, Dr. Watson. The reader only sees, hears, feels, and smells what Dr. Watson sees, hears, feels, and smells. When Sherlock Holmes studies a strange piece of paper found under the cognac glass of the murder victim, Dr. Watson tells us that Holmes's eyes light up, he becomes pensive, he seems to draw some conclusion. Dr. Watson doesn't know what that conclusion is until Holmes tells him at the end of the story, so we don't find out until then, either. If the stories were written with Holmes as the viewpoint character, there would be no mystery.

The reader would not tolerate something like "Holmes studied the mysterious paper with its three red dots and he drew a conclusion."

Holmes knows what his own conclusion is, so it could not be withheld from the reader.

Viewpoint Is Place and Knowledge

In the section on *description*, I noted that the details you choose to mention say, in effect, "This is what the viewpoint character is aware of." That is why happy faces and city music described the viewpoint of a character who had just fallen in love and why sad eyes and a smog-shrouded city described the viewpoint of a character who had just been dumped by his girlfriend.

When you write from a character's point of view, you aren't telling your reader "This is the absolute, unbiased truth." You are telling your reader "The viewpoint character perceives events this way."

The words "My viewpoint character thinks," or "My viewpoint character notices," or "My viewpoint character sees" are always implicit.

If you write "Anita walked into the room. There were cigarette ashes scattered all over the carpet,'' you are really saying "Anita walked into the room. *She saw* that there were cigarette ashes all over the carpet.''

From the viewpoint of a blind character you would not write "The blind man walked into the room. There were cigarette ashes scattered all over the carpet.''

Only write things that the character could know.

Viewpoint is place and knowledge.

Consider this:

Warren Fierst gets a physical examination from Dr. Lydia McMurty. Dr. McMurty breaks the news to him: "Warren, you've got terminal pediculosis, and you'll be lucky to live another six months.'' Warren gets dressed and leaves the doctor's office.

As he walks through the downstairs lobby of the medical building and out onto the street, Warren Fierst's mind is a turmoil of regret. He's going to die, and he feels suddenly as if he's hardly lived. All his adult life has been tied up in work, and he's given little time to people. He has locked in his feelings, his emotions. When he gets out on the sidewalk he spots Kerry O'Donnell walking toward him. Kerry is a longtime friend of Warren's wife, and though Warren has always been fond of her, he's never let those feelings show. He's never hugged her, or kissed her goodnight, never even touched her. Now, caught up in the emotions that he needs to get out before he dies, he rushes toward her and throws his arms around her, clutching her in a desperate, clumsy fashion.

Up at a third-floor window Dr. Lydia McMurty has watched this whole scene, and across the street in an office building Jack Wilson III, a stranger to everyone else, has also been watching.

For various reasons this incident could have taken place in four different stories:

The Dr. Lydia McMurty Story.

The Warren Fierst Story.

The Kerry O'Donnell Story.

The Jack Wilson III Story.

But assuming that each story is written from character viewpoint, the incident will be perceived differently, because each character has a different collection of relevant information.

In The Dr. Lydia McMurty Story, your viewpoint character knows that Warren has just been given a death sentence. You might write:

> From her window Lydia could see Warren as he moved slowly out onto the sidewalk. How he must hurt, she thought, and she wondered if now he would start to show his feelings, now that it was almost too late. Suddenly Warren's pace quickened as he glanced up, and Lydia saw that a woman, apparently a close friend, was coming toward him. The woman started to say something, but in a moment Warren was upon her, hugging her emotionally, sobbing into her shoulder. Lydia felt her heart go out to him.

In The Warren Fierst Story, your viewpoint character knows he is going to die, and he knows there has always been a wall between him and Kerry O'Donnell. You might write:

> When he saw Kerry he rushed to her. He needed her to know that he cared, that he cared deeply about her and all the other friends who had been there for years. He stumbled into her and wrapped his arms around her awkwardly. He wasn't used to hugging people, he knew, and the subtleties of touch were lost to him. But he needed to feel her warmth, to feel the life in her that would continue. He tried to tell her what he was feeling, but no words came out, only sobs.

In The Kerry O'Donnell Story, your viewpoint character does not know about the medical diagnosis, but she does know that Warren Fierst is not an affectionate person. You might write:

A few minutes after she came out of Walgreen's, Kerry

spotted Warren Fierst, Marilyn's husband. Apparently he'd been drinking, for his steps were uncertain and his eyes, when he looked at her, were disturbingly unfocused. Before she could avoid his glance he was all over her, pressing his body against hers in front of everybody. She didn't smell the liquor on his breath, but she knew he was drunk by the way he kept crying her name in slurred, broken syllables. Kerry couldn't stand maudlin drunks at any time, but to be grabbed by one in public like this was humiliating. "Stop it, Warren, stop it," she said, pushing at his shoulder with her hands, but his grip was much too strong.

In The Jack Wilson III Story your viewpoint character doesn't know anything except what he sees. You might write:

Ideas were not coming easily today, so Jack stood by the window for a while, staring out across the city street. He was about to return to his desk when he saw some wacko guy in a business suit attack a woman on the sidewalk. The guy just walked out of the Chandler Building and pounced on the first woman he saw. She screamed at him and tried to push him away, but the guy just held on like a maniac. "The city," Jack thought. "It makes people crazy."

A Viewpoint Game

You have been invited to a Saturday night party at the home of Warren and Marilyn Fierst. I want you to go to the party and write a 400- to 500-word scene describing it.

The following statements are true:

1. On Saturday afternoon Warren Fierst was told by his doctor that he has only six months to live.
2. He has not told anyone yet.
3. There is an attractive young man by the name of Randolph Lehman at the party. He and Marilyn Fierst have been carrying on a secret love affair for a year.

4. Also at the party is Mrs. Dolores Garnet, a woman of about sixty. She has embezzled $100,000 from her employer, and is planning to fly to Argentina in the morning.

5. There is also at the party a fat middle-aged man, Roy Burg, a private detective. He was hired by Dolores Garnet's employer, who knows she stole the money and wants Burg to follow her until she leads him to the cash.

Here's the catch. You don't know any of these facts. All you know is what you see, hear, feel, smell, or taste. But try to write the scene from your viewpoint, hinting at these facts from things that, realistically, you might observe. For example you wouldn't write "As soon as Warren came to the door it was clear to me that he only had six months to live."

But you might write "Warren came to the door. He looked pale and worried. I had to introduce my date twice. Obviously, his thoughts were somewhere else."

Theme

Theme is an aspect of writing not usually found in a section on viewpoint. And yet my dictionary's second definition of *theme* is "An idea, point of view, or perception embodied and expanded upon in a work of art; an underlying or essential subject of artistic representation."

Theme is a mental viewpoint.

There are at least two answers to the question "What is the theme of your story?" One answer is what you look at. The other is how you look at it.

"The theme of my story is young marriage" and "The theme of my story is young marriages make you grow up in a hurry" are both acceptable answers to the question.

Your theme in the second case is your point of view about young marriages. It is your way of looking at them, and though a thousand other writers might have looked at them the same way, it is still *your* point of view.

You should manage your theme with all the care that you use in managing your sensory viewpoint. It should be consistent. The reader should always know where he is in relation to the story: he should know what attitude to take. If he doesn't, then your writing won't work.

There is a dusty old bromide that says if you really have a story, then you can reduce it to a single sentence, such as "A stitch in time saves nine" or "Crying is good for you."

It's true that any story can be reduced to a single sentence, just as any life can be reduced to "Once upon a time a person lived and then died." But it's not necessarily true that the writer knows what the theme sentence is. A writer is not required to put forth a concise statement about his creation any more than an artist or a choreographer is. If you write well and honestly, with character rising from background and action springing from character, and if you remain true to your vision of life, then theme will emerge in the reading process. And if you write what you believe, and only what you believe, the theme will inevitably be consistent.

Slant

If you call up an editor and say, "How would you like an article about houses?" he's going to say, "What about houses?"

The answer to that question is your slant.

It might be, "Lots of people are building underground houses," or "Middle-class people can no longer afford to buy houses," or "Is your house a death trap?" But it will be some specific aspect of houses. Your slant is what makes your article about houses different from mine. It is the aspect of your subject that you choose to look at, and the way you choose to look at it.

Do you remember the interview with Steve Bernstein, the table hockey nut, which I quoted from earlier? From that one interview I sold six articles about Steve Bernstein and/or table hockey. Why? Because each time I took a different slant. I looked at the player and the game in a different way. My mental viewpoint changed.

So slant is also a point of view about a subject. However, you will rarely have the luxury of letting it emerge as you write. For one thing, you need to know your slant ahead of time in order to limit your research. For another, few editors will give you an assignment to write about houses until you answer the question: What about houses?

You

"Can I put myself into my writing?" is one of the questions beginning writers ask most frequently.

The answer is you can't get yourself *out of* your writing. You are there in everything you write. It's just a question of how obvious you are.

Some new writers write about nothing but themselves. Everything they write in class or at home springs from something cute that little Joey said at breakfast or a series of midafternoon calamities involving overflowing Maytags, cars that won't start, and teenagers who keep dialing the wrong number.

Other new writers, terror-stricken at the idea of appearing vain, never mention themselves at all.

Both types of writers make the same mistake. They base the decision about their presence or lack of it in their writing on their ego needs, rather than on what is best for the reader.

Your presence in your writing is neither good nor bad. It's just another tool you have to work with, like verbs, characters, and exclamation points. You can use this tool in many ways to make your writing work, and if you misuse it, your writing will fail.

Before I give you some examples of how your presence can make your writing work, I want to remind you that I am not talking about the "writer at work," who interrupts the reader with his awkward presence. I'm talking about the *personality* whose point of view is deliberately inserted by the writer to one degree or another.

A few months ago my friend Donna Scalcione-Conti and I had articles published in the same magazine. We each inserted ourselves into our articles, but we used the "me" tool in different ways.

Donna began:

Group living is a choice that more and more people are making. The reasons vary. Sometimes they want to save money. Sometimes they prefer living with people of similar interests. Sometimes they seek the closeness of an extended family.

I chose group living for all of those reasons, but the longer I live this lifestyle, the more advantages I discover.

About a year ago my children, Erica, 8, and Nicky, 6, and I moved in with three close friends—Gary and Nora, a married couple, and Jim, a single parent whose two children visit on weekends.

From this point on, everything Donna wrote concerned her particular situation. How the people in *her* house managed group living, how *her* kids received extra attention from the four adults, how *she* saved money, and so on. But she was not just idly publishing pages from her diary. Every aspect of group living that she dealt with was one that would come up in Juneau, El Paso, or Elgin, Illinois.

She told universal truths about group living by using herself as an example. What she did was no different from tracking down an extended family living in a group home somewhere and focusing a "group living" article on them. The home she chose happened to be her own.

My article began:

There is an acre of woods not far from the house, and sometimes when Donna and I stroll down these suburban back streets to reach those woods, we hold hands.

Our neighbors never take walks. But sometimes they are around, puttering with cantankerous engines or squinting out at the day through living room curtains.

"Out for their morning walk," they think when they see us. And they think, too, that we are married. Or lovers. Or maybe, just maybe, brother and sister. It's true. I'm sure of it.

I'm also sure that I find it odd that it never occurs to them that a man and woman holding hands might be friends.

But friends we are. She is the mother of two. I am the husband of one. And we are joyously caught up in that most enduring and least trumpeted of relationships these days, the close personal friendship.

In another world, another time, we might have been lovers. For the here and now we are the bearers of that most ignominious label: "just friends."

Just friends. The phrase is an affront to anybody who loves a friend of the opposite sex. It assumes that friendship is a second-class relationship. But there is nothing diminutive about friendship between a man and a woman. It needs no *just* to explain it.

What it does need is understanding. And fast. The feminist movement and a depressed economy have combined to drag male-female friendships out of the closet and toss them into offices, classrooms, kitchens and, yes, bedrooms.

At this point *I* left the article completely and never reappeared until the final paragraph. The bulk of the piece was about the

phenomenon of male-female friendships and how they are growing closer and more open and acceptable.

I used myself as a friendly person leading the reader into a
touchy subject. I used myself and Donna as an opening anecdote,
just as I might have used two people I had met in my research.
And I used myself to make my article more credible. The reader
knows that the author is involved in a close opposite-sex friendship and thus is more inclined to accept the author's views on the
subject.

Though Donna and I use our selves in different ways in our
articles, it is clear in both cases that we are there.

Now consider this excerpt from an article I wrote about a local
psychic:

> While the psychics might read much of the same material,
> each interprets and sorts it out to suit his own experience.
> One man's ultimate metaphysical truth is another man's
> hogwash.
>
> Even when things do mean something, the struggle to
> communicate is one endemic to the psychic. He is trying to
> put across a body of information that is never the same thing
> twice. He is trying to describe experiences that might not
> have happened to the people who make up words, and often,
> in doing so, he must resort to words that have not earned
> their way into any dictionaries.
>
> While the public may perceive the psychic simply as a
> mind reader or a clairvoyant, more often he is a general
> dabbler in the occult. Mal Brown's monologues, for exam-
> ple, are a potpourri of almost everything that is strange.

There is no *I* or *me* in that article, but the writer is clearly
present. My *point of view* is all over that piece in a way that
would be different if I were a disciple of the occult or an immov-
able skeptic. My choice of words, my choice of incidents, all
reflect my point of view. You cannot write a totally objective

article for the same reason you cannot write objective description or create objective characterization. *You can't write everything. You have to make choices, and as soon as you choose this instead of that, you have ceased to treat all things equally.* Since anything you write is made up entirely of your choices, you can never get yourself completely out of your writing.

But that's not a bad thing. Don't be afraid to put yourself into your articles. Your point of view is one of the things you have to sell. If writers didn't inject their points of view, everything could be written by a computer. Writers could be put on pension and exiled to Martha's Vineyard.

Your point of view and your writing skills are all you have to sell. Make both work for you.

Part

EIGHT

Some Closing Words

A couple of nights ago as I neared the end of this book, I took a few hours off and went out to have a drink with my friend Ron Trahan, who is also a writer. Ron has been selling freelance articles for a couple of years while working at a full-time job. Like all writers, he dreams of bigger things. He dreams of making it big as a writer, of getting to the point where he can earn all of his living from writing. During the last two months Ron finally got together enough energy, hope, and time to put together a book query, some sample chapters, and an outline for a book about careers with horses. It has been the focus of his hopes as a writer.

One reason he needed to be with me this particular night was that he was going through that painful, hopeful period of waiting to hear from a book publisher. Would they want him or not? Would they accept him as a writer, or would they send his material back? The book sale, more than anything else, is the symbolic point at which a person can say "I have made it as a writer." When a writer is wrestling with these feelings he turns to another writer. Sometimes another writer understands what the rest of the world does not.

Ron is also a photographer, and while we sat in the lounge talking shop he offered to take photos of me to be used in promoting this book, and maybe for the cover.

"I want to do something good," he said. "I want to capture you and your book the way you see it. So think about what you are trying to say with the book, and I'll have a better sense of what to do with the photos."

Ron meant I should think it over and come back to him in three days, but my answer came right out.

"When I started this book," I said, "I wanted to take some of the phoniness out of writing. I wanted to rub away the magic and show new writers that writing for publication is real. They could approach it. It could be learned, just as good photography can be learned. And I also wanted them to see that the answers weren't confined to any one place. You can learn to write in college, but you can also learn in the public library, in local adult education classes, in writers' magazines.

"I never went to college," I said. "I barely got out of high school, and yet I learned to write and people pay me money to write. Imagine two boxers. One of them learned to fight out on the street by getting in scraps and now and then getting his face kicked in. The other went to some fancy-Dan boxing academy where he learned 'the right way.' I guess I want to say that the only 'right way' is the way that works, and if it doesn't capture the reader, then by definition it's wrong, no matter how good the grammar or how perfect the punctuation."

Ron smiled. "You're a street writer," he said. "That's what you are, a street writer," and he started sketching out photo ideas on a napkin. He understood.

Sometimes another writer understands what the rest of the world does not.

As I sat down to write these final words, several recent conversations like this one with writers and writing students came to me. They all seemed to contain some germ of encouragement I could pass on to you. Except one.

And something keeps telling me to pass on to you just that one other recent conversation, the one that wasn't so positive. It was painful.

Ruth is a woman in one of my classes. I don't know how old she is. Middle fifties, I would guess. During a class coffee break two weeks ago she told me that when she was twenty-one years old she wrote a story and sent it to a confession magazine. She haunted the mailbox for weeks, as writers do, and one day a check arrived. They had bought her story. Her lofty dream of becoming a published writer had come true. She was ecstatic. The world was suddenly a hopeful place, and she could see the possibility of an exciting writing career stretching out before her.

She never published another word.

When I asked her why, she said it was because her family and friends made fun of her. "Are you writing for those sleazy magazines?" they said. They embarrassed her. They made her feel bad about her writing.

I suspect that it is not just what her family and friends did, but also what they didn't do, that kept Ruth from ever submitting another manuscript.

They didn't praise her.

They didn't congratulate her.

They didn't tell her she had done something valuable.

But she *had* done something valuable. She had written something and shared it. There is nothing sleazy about writing a story that somebody somewhere will enjoy. There is nothing sleazy about committing your vision of life to paper. There is nothing sleazy about setting out to accomplish the difficult and accomplishing it.

I cannot tell you how angry I am with people like Ruth's family. I don't suppose it would rankle me so if it were an isolated case. But it's not. I hear the same thing over and over again from my students.

"My husband doesn't take much interest in my writing."

"My wife never reads what I write."

"The kids think I'm crazy to sit at a typewriter all day."

Don't ever . . . ever . . . let someone convince you that your writing is not important. If it's important to you, then it is important. Don't let anybody tell you that a story published in the *Atlantic* is valuable, but one published in *Modern Romances* is not. If a reader finds something of value in what you write, then it is valuable, no matter who found it or where.

And when the husband and the wife and the kids and the parents and the so-called friends are all deaf to your need to be heard as a writer . . . find another writer. Take a class. Put an ad in the paper. Call up someone whose byline you see. Accost people on the street and say, "Are you a writer? I am." Do what you have to, but find another writer.

Sometimes another writer understands what the rest of the world does not.

I know it has been said a million times, but I must say this again because it has been so true in my life and in the lives of writers I've known: Nothing takes the place of persistence.

Keep on writing and reading and writing and taking classes and writing and sending manuscripts out and writing and learning and writing. Persistence.

If you don't believe me, ask Ron Trahan.

Few things in life happen right on cue, but this time something did. The day after Ron and I had that drink and that conversation, just when I needed some encouraging event with which to end this book, Ron got a phone call. From a major book publisher. They want his book. He signs the contract next week. He has made it as a writer.

Giving up doesn't work.

Persistence works.

Make every word count.

INDEX